REAL STORIES

BOOK 2

Woman Mayor

NEW BRUNSWICK, N.J., May 31 (UPI)—When Patricia Sheehan, 33 years old, widowed mother of 3 children, became mayor of this *historic* city with a *population* of 40,000 she found out a number of interesting things:

Being a mayor, a mother and holding still another job calls for more time than there is in a 24-hour day.

Among her other duties as mayor, she must be *available to perform* weddings.

Her friends are *confused* about what to call her. "Hello, Pat . . . er, I mean, Mrs. Mayor . . . er, I mean, Your Honor."

City Hall was so unprepared for a woman, it took her several days to get a key to the ladies' room.

"I understand," said Mrs. Sheehan, "that I am one of the few women mayors and that I may be the youngest. I do know that I've had letters of *congratulations* from all over the country.

"I still haven't figured out how I'm going to *juggle* all my jobs, but I've always been a busy person," she said. "That'll help. The mayor's job was made to be part-time, you know."

Terry. He called and in a short while Pamela was sitting in her home with her sister and two brothers.

Pamela and Terry discovered that they had been sitting in nearby booths the night Mr. and Mrs. Talmadge took her out to a restaurant to *celebrate* the Miss Indiana title. Terry's wife even *commented* on the pretty girl across the *aisle*.

BLIND BOWLER

Is blindness the worst thing that can happen a person?

Many of the bowlers their alleys in the middle games and lined up thr and four deep to watch short, barrel-chested, S year-old man take four st and swiftly roll a bowl ball. The crowd was plain surprised at the speed a *accuracy* of the ball a broke into loud *applause* the pins fell.

Joe Feinberg, who cann see the pins fall because is blind, hears each *ovatic*

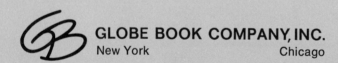

GLOBE BOOK COMPANY, INC.
New York   Chicago

e claps his hands, does a
tle dance and smiles like a
ung bowler who has just
lled his first strike.

With over 50 *trophies* to
s credit. Mr. Feinberg is
e of the most famous blind
owlers in the United States.

In a National Blind Bowl-
s Tournament in Cincin-
ti, Mr. Feinberg's three-
ame series of 580 (184,
2, 194) was the highest
ore of the 700 bowlers
ompeting in the *event*.

Mr. Feinberg bowls more
an 20 games a day at any
ne of 20 Brooklyn lanes to
hich he has a standing in-
tation. His way of bowling
unusual among the blind

Almost all blind bowlers
se a rail that leads them
ong the *approach* to the
ley. Mr. Feinberg uses
Continued on Page 34, Col. 2

THE CHEFS' FINAL EXAM

How would you like to eat
your final exam?

Final exams for 17 stu-
dents of Milwaukee Institute
of Technology were held
one morning this week in
Room 662. Two long tables,
covered with fresh, white
linen and decorated with
white lilac, held nine dessert
items and eight *entree*
courses, each carefully *labeled*.

Starting with the entrees.
the mouth-watering list

Mrs. Sheehan will be re-
sponsible for a budget of
$9,000,000 a year. Her own
salary is $5,500 a year

At home, her phone keeps
ringing, her children come
home from school full of
stories of the day's happenings, a neighbor stops in to
say, "Pat . . . er. Your Hon-
or, I can't drive our children

read: "Chateaubriand with
Mushroom Sauce," "Filet de
Sole Marguery," "Roast
Duckling," "Sautéed Breast
of Chicken on Toast Points,"
"Sauerbraten," "Roast Cor-
nish Hen," "Chicken Kiev

real
stories

book 2

Milton Katz

Michael Chakeres   ### Murray Bromberg

Second Edition 1975

ISBN: 0-87065-205-2

This edition may be used with all
other editions, in the same classroom,
without conflict of any kind.

Illustrations by Harry J. Schaare
Cover design by Lawrence Schaeffer
Text design by Edward Zytko

8 9

ABOUT THE AUTHORS

MILTON KATZ, the chairman of English at Thomas Jefferson High School, Brooklyn, N.Y., has been a high school reading coordinator and a program writer for the Responsive Environment Center. He was the editor of *Moonlight Review*, a national teachers' literary magazine. Mr. Katz holds the degrees of B.A. from Brooklyn College and M.A. from New York University.

MICHAEL CHAKERES, an expert in the field of reading and reading curriculum development, is presently a reading consultant in the High School Reading Program, Board of Education, City of New York. He holds a Secondary School Principal's license from New York State and has been laboratory supervisor and coordinator of the Responsive Environment Program.

MURRAY BROMBERG has taught English and been Chairman of English at Thomas Jefferson High School, Brooklyn, New York. Mr. Bromberg has also taught at Hofstra University. Now principal of Andrew Jackson High School, Queens, New York, he is a contributing author of several books including Globe's *Our American Language, Biography for Youth, World-Wide Essays* and *Literature of Mystery: Four Representative Types*. He has published articles in *Shakespeare Quarterly* and other periodicals. Mr. Bromberg holds the degrees of B.A. from Brooklyn College and M.A. from Columbia University.

ACKNOWLEDGMENTS

For permission to reprint copyrighted materials, grateful acknowledgment is made to the following publishers and news services:

"Two-Minute Tornado" reprinted with permission of *The Denver Post*.

"Coincidence" reprinted with permission of *The Courier-Journal* and *The Louisville Times*.

"Teen-Age Eating Habits" reprinted with permission from SCIENCE NEWS (formerly titled SCIENCE NEWS LETTER) weekly summary of current science, copyright © 1965 by Science Service, Inc.

"High-Flying High School Courses," copyright © 1967 by The New York Times Company. Reprinted by permission.

"Sinkholes," copyright © 1967 by The New York Times Company. Reprinted by permission.

"Turkish Town Talks in Whistles," copyright © 1964 by The New York Times Company. Reprinted by permission.

"Drop-Out Veteran Gets Diploma" reprinted with permission of *The Milwaukee Journal*.

"Blind Bowler," copyright © 1964 by The New York Times Company. Reprinted by permission.

"Rescue by Human Chain" reprinted with permission from Newsday, Inc.

"Girl in a Man's World" reprinted courtesy of *The News,* New York's Picture Newspaper.

"Woman Mayor" reprinted with permission of the *St. Louis Post-Dispatch*.

"New Ways to Fight Crime" reprinted with permission of *The Times-Union*.

CONTENTS

ABOUT THE BOOK

At some point in our own lives, each of us has listened to or told stories. Some were made up; others were true-to-fact—real. We all have our private "fish tale" about the one that got away. We all have our personal experiences that we share with relatives and friends.

REAL STORIES, BOOK II, presents twenty-five true-to-fact stories about real people and real events. All of them were adapted from newspapers and magazines. Each of them was chosen to entertain you and arouse your curiosity.

Two of the real people are Jim McMillan and Danny Fernandez. Jim was the hero of Columbia University's basketball team; Danny, a war hero who gave his life that others might live. Other real stories highlight a woman mayor, a girl auto racer, and a blind FBI agent.

The human side of real events is brought out in "Rescue by Human Chain"—an event which brings men together to save a busload of trapped youngsters. Other real events describe the effects of natural disasters as explored in "Sinkholes," and the spirit of man as talked about in "The Thinking Machine."

We have all listened to or told stories. Some were made up; others were true-to-fact—real. Now, let's *read* stories—REAL STORIES.

1. TWO-MINUTE TORNADO

WHAT IS A TORNADO?

WHAT IS THE FIRST THING YOU WOULD DO IF A TORNADO STRUCK YOUR HOME?

DENVER, Colo., June 10—A tornado hit East Denver yesterday and left the people of the area amazed by its force.

Thomas Williams was sitting on his porch shortly before noon when the storm hit. He went into his house when it started to rain and then went back out to see if his chair was going to be *soaked* by the rain.

"I opened the door," he said, "and it sounded like a *locomotive* was going to come in. It *roared* and whistled and I closed the door. In two minutes it was all over. I didn't have time to be scared."

Williams said the tornado took out two large spruce trees behind his house and three trees in front. His home was hit by a roof from the house two doors away.

His neighbor, George Bryant, was painting his house when it got dark and started to rain and hail.

"My wife thought the *furnace* was *exploding* because of the noise and dirt in the air," Bryant

1

said. "My wife and son ran into the basement. I went out to close the garage door.

"When I grabbed the door, the tornado came along and lifted me and the door right up in the air. I let go and ran into the basement."

He said that the tornado had a *high-pitched,* whistling sound that was *eerie.*

The tornado took out the kitchen window and bedroom window, and *split* the kitchen door down the middle. It also ripped all the tile off the front of the roof.

Little is known about why a tornado starts. There is no good way of warning people in the path of a tornado. A tornado, unlike a hurricane, is so *brief* that it is almost *impossible* to find out very much about it.

—DENVER POST

CHECK YOUR UNDERSTANDING

1. Another title that would best explain the main idea of this story is:
   (a) A Dangerous Hailstorm
   (b) A Powerful Storm
   (c) Thomas Williams' Porch
   (d) The Power of a Locomotive
2. Thomas Williams went outside again after the storm hit because
   (a) he wanted to see if his chair had been soaked.
   (b) he was scared.

(c) he heard a locomotive.

(d) his house was hit by a roof from the house two doors away.

3. Mr. Bryant
   (a) was in the basement when the storm struck.
   (b) was almost lifted into the air by the tornado.
   (c) was hanging onto a spruce tree.
   (d) was sitting on his porch before the storm struck.

4. A tornado is dangerous because
   (a) it strikes in the dark.
   (b) it can damage or destroy things in its way.
   (c) it can scare people.
   (d) it lasts a long time.

5. Little is known about tornadoes because
   (a) they are too powerful to check on.
   (b) planes will not fly when a tornado strikes.
   (c) they are over very quickly.
   (d) they do not happen often.

REACHING OUT

1. A tornado does *not* have
   (a) high winds.
   (b) roaring sounds like a locomotive.
   (c) whistling noises.
   (d) a long life.

2. The tornado in the story did *not*
   (a) take out two large spruce trees from behind the Williams' house.
   (b) split the Bryants' kitchen door.

(c) explode the furnace in the Bryant house.

(d) take out the kitchen window of the Bryant house.

SIGHTS AND SOUNDS

The good reader not only uses his imagination to see things that happen in a story, but also remembers the sounds. Pick out the words in the second column that finish either the picture or the sound started by the words in the first column.

A	**B**
1. The tornado	(a) was eerie.
2. Mr. Bryant's wife	(b) roared and whistled like a locomotive.
3. The high-pitched whistle Mr. Bryant heard	(c) heard a noise like an explosion and thought that the furnace blew up.
4. Mr. Bryant and the garage door	(d) was hit by a roof.
5. The Williams' house	(e) were lifted right up in the air.

IMPROVING YOUR VOCABULARY

In the first column below are the ten words in italics from the story. Pick out the best "story" meaning for each of these words.

1. *soaked* by the rain (a) made very wet; (b) dried; (c) covered

2. a speeding *locomotive* — (a) a car; (b) a train engine; (c) a speedboat

3. *roared* like a lion — (a) raced; (b) jumped; (c) made a loud, deep noise

4. *furnace* for heat — (a) a pot; (b) wood; (c) something in which to make a fire

5. *exploding* noises — (a) blowing up; (b) separate; (c) faraway

6. *high-pitched* sound — (a) up in the air; (b) shrill, like a scream; (c) very funny

7. *eerie* sound — (a) low; (b) normal; (c) strange

8. *split* the wood — (a) cut from end to end; (b) let fall; (c) pile up

9. *brief* as a minute — (a) average; (b) short; (c) long

10. *impossible* to find — (a) not able to be done; (b) not to be lost; (c) not to be passed

---

WORD BUILDING

The word *exploding* from the story above means *blowing up*. The meanings of the different parts of the word will give you a hint about how the word has come to mean *blowing up*.

> Explanation: The prefix *ex* means *out* or *from*. The stem *plode* means to *drive*. The suffix *ing* changes the word from *explode* to *exploding*.

Put the first two parts of the word back together.

The word *explode* means to *drive out*.

Add *ing*.

The word *exploding* means *driving out*.

Whenever you see *ex* at the start of a word, it means *out* or *from*.

Example: *exit* means to *go out*.

To Do: Match the word in column B with the proper *ex* word in column A.

A	**B**
1. The United States *exports* machinery to many countries.	(a) change from one to another
2. During the Christmas season many people *exchange* gifts.	(b) sends out
	(c) leaving out
	(d) stirred
3. The fans were *excited* when their local hero caught the winning touchdown pass.	(e) told; described
4. He answered all the questions *except* the last one.	
5. He *explained* how he solved the problem.	

EXPRESSING YOURSELF

1. Man has always had to fight against some of the dangerous forces of nature, such as tornadoes, earthquakes, volcanoes, floods, hurri-

canes, fire, lightning, disease, quicksand, sink-holes, and wild animals. Write a paragraph about something that happened to you or someone you know in facing one or more of these dangers.

2. Would you rather be in a tornado or a hurricane? Look up these subjects in an encyclopedia before you answer.

3. In the story, *The Wizard of Oz,* Dorothy is picked up by a tornado and carried to the enchanted land of Oz. Where would you like to land if a tornado picked you up? Why?

4. Describe three dangerous forces in nature and how they can cause damage.

2. COINCIDENCE

A COINCIDENCE IS SOMETHING THAT DOESN'T SEEM VERY LIKELY TO HAPPEN, YET DOES.

TWO STUDENTS MIGHT HAVE PERFECT ATTENDANCE RECORDS FOR YEARS AND THEN BE ABSENT ON THE VERY SAME DAY. IN THE STORY YOU ARE ABOUT TO READ, PAMELA TALMADGE HAD AN UNUSUAL COINCIDENCE.

HAMMOND, Ind. (UPI)—The night last April when Pamela Talmadge was crowned Miss

Indiana, her brother was sitting only a few feet from her. But she did not know it. And he did not know the *stunning brunette* was his sister.

Pamela, 20, was *adopted* when she was six months old. Later, she was told that she had two brothers and a sister, but she could not find them.

When Pamela *competed* in the Miss Universe contest as Miss Indiana, her brothers and sister saw her picture, *remarked* on a family likeness, but thought no more of it.

But Pamela and her family were *united* Tuesday night because Francis Talmadge, the man who had adopted her, would not stop looking. Talmadge knew Pamela wanted to see the members of her family and he set out to find them.

"I *searched* and hunted for 11 years, always running into blind alleys," he said.

Talmadge checked telephone books in every city he visited. Two weeks ago in Cicero, Illinois, he found the name of Pamela's brother, Terry. He called and in a short while Pamela was sitting in her home with her sister and two brothers.

Pamela and Terry discovered that they had been sitting in nearby booths the night Mr. and Mrs. Talmadge took her out to a restaurant to *celebrate* the Miss Indiana title. Terry's wife even *commented* on the pretty girl across the *aisle*.

"Imagine, only a few feet away," Pamela said. "And my 'father' and I had been searching for years."

—LOUISVILLE COURIER-JOURNAL

CHECK YOUR UNDERSTANDING

1. Another title that would best explain the main idea of this story is:
   (a) Pamela Talmadge's Victory
   (b) Together, After Twenty Years
   (c) The Miss Universe Contest
   (d) Terry Talmadge
2. When Pamela's family saw her picture, they
   (a) recognized her immediately.
   (b) saw no family likeness.
   (c) thought she looked like other members of the family.
   (d) thought she was beautiful.
3. Mr. Talmadge was able to help Pamela find her family because
   (a) he knew her brother Terry.
   (b) he searched carefully in every city he visited.
   (c) he sent out a picture of her to the newspapers.
   (d) she had won the Miss Universe contest.
4. Pamela was separated from her family for
   (a) 14 years.
   (b) most of her life.
   (c) a few months.
   (d) the Miss Universe contest.
5. The expression, "running into a blind alley," means
   (a) the starting point.
   (b) a dark place.
   (c) a special street for blind people.

10

(d) reaching a point in your search where there is no more information.

REACHING OUT

1. Francis Talmadge did *not*
   (a) search for 11 years to find Pamela's family.
   (b) take Pamela to a restaurant to celebrate her victory in the beauty contest.
   (c) arrange for the family to meet in a restaurant.
   (d) check the telephone book to find Pamela's family.
2. A coincidence happened when
   (a) Pamela sat next to her brother without knowing it.
   (b) Pamela's sister saw her picture in the newspaper.
   (c) Mr. Talmadge found Terry's name in the newspaper.
   (d) Pamela took part in the Miss Universe contest.

FIRST THINGS FIRST

Arrange these events in the same order as they happened in the story.
1. Pamela won the Miss Indiana beauty contest.
2. Pamela discovered that her brother had sat next to her on the day she won the Miss Indiana contest.
3. Pamela met her brothers and sister.

4. Mr. Talmadge found Terry's telephone number in the directory.
5. Mr. Talmadge planned to check telephone books in every city that he visited.
6. Pamela took part in the Miss Universe contest.
7. Pamela's family saw a family likeness in her picture.

IMPROVING YOUR VOCABULARY

In the column below are the ten italicized words from the story. Pick out the best "story" meaning for each of these words.

1. *stunning* looks — (a) very good-looking; (b) unpleasant; (c) angry

2. a *brunette* — (a) person from Northern Italy; (b) beauty-contest winner; (c) a person with dark brown or black hair

3. *adopted* child — (a) best-loved; (b) only; (c) taken as one's own

4. *competed* in a contest — (a) took part in a contest; (b) won first prize; (c) was the judge

5. *remarked* on the likeness — (a) sat silently; (b) spoke; (c) spoke loudly

6. family was *united* — (a) separated; (b) had dinner at home; (c) brought together

7. he *searched* for her — (a) tried to do his best; (b) looked for; (c) was lonesome

8. went to *celebrate*	(a) look closely at; (b) try for a prize; (c) enjoy a special occasion
9. she *commented*	(a) spoke; (b) grew angry; (c) looked silly
10. girl across the *aisle*	(a) island; (b) open space between rows of seats; (c) back row of a theater

---

WORD BUILDING

The word *unite* is used in the story above. It means to bring together.

Unite is built from two word parts: *uni* is a prefix which means *one,* and *ite* is a stem which means *part.* Can you see how the idea of *one part* could come to mean *to bring together?*

Usually, when you see *uni* at the start of a word, it has the meaning of *one.*

Example: A *unicycle* is a bicycle with only *one* wheel.

To Do: Match the meaning in column B to the proper *uni* word in column A.

A	**B**
1. *uniform* material	(a) bring together; make one
2. a *union* of states	
3. *unite* different groups	(b) made into one
4. *united* nations	(c) of the same quality
5. an army *unit*	(d) one part of a whole
	(e) a joining together

13

A Little Harder: Match the word in column B to the proper *uni* word in column A.

A	B
1. *unanimous* vote	(a) as one voice
2. *unique* art work	(b) one-sided
3. sang in *unison*	(c) only one of its kind
4. *unilateral* action	(d) throughout the world
5. *universal* custom	(e) agreed to by all

EXPRESSING YOURSELF

1. At a dance, you discover that your partner's father works for the same company as your father. Make up other coincidences which might take place:
   (a) at the beach.
   (b) on a bus.
   (c) in the lunchroom.

2. You have a dream about a friend you haven't seen or thought about for years. Then, the very next day, you meet that friend. Is that a coincidence, or would you explain it differently?

3. Some people believe that human lives are controlled by the stars. These people believe in "astrology." They can read their "horoscopes" in newspapers. These horoscopes are written by astrologers who claim they can tell the future by studying where the stars and planets are. Tell whether or not you believe in astrology. Give reasons for your opinion.

4. Write a paragraph about a coincidence that happened to you or someone you know.

3. TEEN-AGE EATING HABITS

WHAT DO YOU USUALLY EAT FOR BREAKFAST? WHAT DO YOU THINK OF YOUR EATING HABITS?

FIND OUT HOW YOU COMPARE WITH STUDENTS IN GREENSBORO, NORTH CAROLINA.

Teen-agers are not eating enough lettuce, carrots, tomatoes, and other vegetables. They're also not eating as much fruit as they should.

15

Only about one out of six teen-agers daily have those green leafy and yellow vegetables so *vital* for their growing bodies.

A *survey* was made of the food *habits* of 6200 boys and girls from the junior and senior high schools in Greensboro, North Carolina. It was found that the older the student, the more meals he or she missed. Students in the seventh grade missed 10% of their meals. By the time students reached the twelfth grade, they were missing 25% of their meals.

Although a *majority* of the students ate breakfast, more students in the high school grades missed this important meal than those in the junior high school grades.

Eating breakfast is important. It has been found that students who miss breakfast *generally* do poorer in school.

Younger students often chose more *wholesome snacks* in the mid-mornings and mid-afternoons. They *preferred* milk, fruit, bread, and cereals, while older students chose soft drinks and candies to *curb* their hunger.

Generally, the more a student knows about good eating habits, the better his eating habits *actually* are.

—SCIENCE NEWS

CHECK YOUR UNDERSTANDING

1. Another title that would best explain the main idea of this story is:

   (a) Teen-Age Diet Needs Improvement

(b) The Importance of Eating Breakfast

(c) Eating Habits of Older Students

(d) Teen-Agers Prefer Fruit

2. Most of the students
   (a) had a snack of green vegetables daily.
   (b) ate enough fruit.
   (c) missed breakfast.
   (d) ate breakfast.

3. The older students
   (a) preferred milk to soda.
   (b) always ate breakfast.
   (c) had better eating habits than younger students.
   (d) missed more meals than younger students.

4. Younger students
   (a) liked soft drinks and candy for snacks.
   (b) often missed breakfast.
   (c) chose more healthy snacks than older students.
   (d) ate vegetables daily.

5. According to the story, if a student misses breakfast,
   (a) it does not affect his ability to work.
   (b) it helps him in his school work.
   (c) he feels better about school in general.
   (d) it may affect his ability to work.

REACHING OUT

1. An important food not mentioned in the story is
   (a) vegetables.
   (b) meat.
   (c) tomatoes.
   (d) fruit.

2. According to the selection, which of the following statements is true?
  - (a) Older students in Greensboro, North Carolina, have better eating habits than younger students.
  - (b) Younger students in Greensboro, North Carolina, have better eating habits than older students.
  - (c) Knowing about good eating habits has no influence on proper diet.
  - (d) Knowing about good eating habits usually leads to better eating habits.

GETTING THE NUMBER FACTS

In your reading you are constantly faced with "number facts" which you must understand. A good reader can remember what he reads because the number facts make sense. This exercise is designed to help you get the number facts. The questions are based on the number facts in the story.

1. How many boys and girls were studied in the survey?

2. What *per cent* of their meals do students in the twelfth grade miss?

3. If twelfth-grade students were supposed to eat 100 meals, how many meals might they miss?

4. What *per cent* of their meals do students in the seventh grade miss?

5. If seventh-grade students were supposed to eat 100 meals, how many meals would they probably miss?

6. If a majority of one hundred students eat breakfast, at least how many of the students must eat breakfast?
7. If one out of six youngsters eats green leafy and yellow vegetables, how many youngsters do not?

IMPROVING YOUR VOCABULARY

In the first column below are the ten words in italics from the story. Pick out the best "story" meaning for each of these words.

1. *vital* for growth — (a) necessary; (b) painful; (c) filling
2. *survey* of students — (a) total among; (b) study; (c) cost
3. dangerous smoking *habits* — (a) practices; (b) types; (c) diets
4. *majority* of the class — (a) less than half; (b) two; (c) more than half
5. *generally* do poorer — (a) a lot; (b) for the most part; (c) great
6. *wholesome* food — (a) large piece; (b) spoiled; (c) healthful
7. tasty *snacks* — (a) light meals; (b) heavy meals; (c) drinks
8. *preferred* candy — (a) liked less; (b) liked more; (c) cared about
9. *curb* their hunger — (a) hold back; (b) eat a lot; (c) park
10. the better you *actually* are — (a) of course; (b) by the way; (c) in fact

WORD BUILDING

The word *preferred* from the story above means *chose before* something else. When we say that the students in the survey preferred milk, fruit, bread, and cereals, we mean that they chose them before some other food. The part of the word *preferred* which you should remember is *pre*. It means *before*.

To Do: Write the meaning of each of the following *pre* words. The first one is done for you.

1. prearrange—to arrange before
2. pretest
3. prejudge
4. preview
5. preheat

A Little Harder: Match the meaning in column B to the proper *pre* word in column A.

A	B
1. *preface* of a book	(a) before written history
2. take every *precaution*	(b) to tell before it happens
3. *predict* the score	(c) a part of the word placed before the stem
4. *prehistoric* man	(d) care taken before
5. the *prefix* of a word	(e) the introduction or part of the book that comes first

EXPRESSING YOURSELF

1. Tell about your good eating habits and your poor eating habits. How can you improve on your poor eating habits?
2. You have decided to make the most delicious meal in the world. Tell what foods you would buy and how you would prepare them.
3. Imagine that the school dietician has asked students to tell her how they feel about the menus for next week. Make a list of your ideas for a full week of great eating in your school's lunchroom.
4. How do the eating habits of some other countries differ from American eating habits? Use an encyclopedia to help you answer.

4. HIGH-FLYING HIGH SCHOOL COURSES

DO YOU THINK HIGH SCHOOLS SHOULD HAVE A COURSE IN FLYING?

THIS STORY MAY MAKE YOU WANT SUCH A COURSE IN YOUR SCHOOL.

At least 100 high schools in the United States now have courses in *aviation* for those students who want to take such a course.

Many grade schools also have aviation courses.

In one such course, the teacher helps the pupils to learn about flying by taking them on a make-believe cross-country *flight*. They *discuss* the airplane's parts, the way an airplane is put together, what makes it fly, and how it is flown.

The pupils map the course of flight, check the winds, and figure the speed and time of takeoff and *arrival*. They may *detour* because of storm clouds. In case they get "lost," they learn to find out where they are by using the plane's radio. By the time the students have "landed," they have had an exciting time, learned a lot about how an airplane works, and have also learned a little geography, mathematics, and weather science.

Many high schools *offer* flying lessons along with *instruction* in how an airplane works. Three high schools in Atlanta, Georgia, for example, now have *permanent* aviation courses and offer flying lessons at $9 an hour.

Some schools even own their own planes. One such school is in Crescent City, California. It gives students in its aviation courses two free hours of flight *training*. Afterwards, the rates are $2 an hour for the first ten hours and $4 an hour for the next 40 hours. It would cost the student about $15 an hour if he tried to get this flying instruction from a private flying school.

Many of the students in the high school aviation courses take the Federal Aviation Administration's written test to become a private *pilot*. A good number go on to pick up flying licenses by passing the second part of the test, a solo flight, when they fly a plane alone over a test area.

—NEW YORK TIMES

CHECK YOUR UNDERSTANDING

1. Another title that would best explain the main idea of this story is:
   (a) Make-Believe Flying
   (b) How Airplanes Work
   (c) Aviation Courses in Public Schools
   (d) Learning to Fly
2. If a student wanted private flying lessons, it would cost him about
   (a) $2 an hour.
   (b) $4 an hour.
   (c) $9 an hour.
   (d) $15 an hour.
3. To receive a private pilot's license a student must
   (a) own an airplane.
   (b) pass a written and solo-flight test.
   (c) take flying courses in high school.
   (d) go to one of three high schools in Atlanta, Georgia.
4. All the high schools in the United States that have aviation courses
   (a) own their own planes.
   (b) give free flying lessons.
   (c) give flying lessons for a fee of $9 an hour.
   (d) offer instruction in how an airplane works.

REACHING OUT

1. Pupils in grade school do *not*
   (a) learn to guide a plane along its course of flight.

24

(b) fly their own planes.

(c) know how to read maps.

(d) learn how to use a plane's radio.

2. Which of the following is *not* true?

(a) Public schools that offer flying lessons usually charge their students a small fee.

(b) High school students can take flying lessons.

(c) High school students receive their pilot's license as soon as they finish their course.

(d) It is less expensive to take flying lessons in a public school than from a private flying school.

PUTTING THE PIECES TOGETHER

Below is a title for each of the six paragraphs in the story. Put these titles in the same order as the paragraphs in the story.

1. High School Flying Instruction
2. The Cost of Flying Lessons
3. Grade Schools and Flying Courses
4. What Grade School Students Learn about Flying
5. How to Get a Private Pilot's License
6. The Number of Aviation Courses in U.S. High Schools

IMPROVING YOUR VOCABULARY

In the first column below are the ten words in italics from the story. Pick out the best "story" meaning for each of these words.

1. courses in *aviation* — (a) science of flying airplanes; (b) the history of a country; (c) weather science
2. cross-country *flight* — (a) boxing match; (b) fear; (c) air travel
3. *discuss* the problem — (a) answer; (b) throw; (c) talk over
4. plane's *arrival* — (a) enemy; (b) landing; (c) leaving
5. make a *detour* — (a) roundabout way; (b) short trip; (c) visit
6. *offer* flying lessons — (a) to buy; (b) to present; (c) to take
7. music *instruction* — (a) wrecking; (b) playing; (c) teaching
8. *permanent* courses — (a) not lasting; (b) lasting; (c) hair-cutting
9. business *training* — (a) practical learning; (b) building a train; (c) enjoying a hobby
10. *pilot* of a boat — (a) passenger; (b) fireman; (c) person who steers

---

WORD BUILDING

The word *instruction* from the story above means *teaching*. Let's look at the parts of the word to see how it got this meaning. There are three parts in the word: *in* means *on; struc(t)* means *to build* or *building; tion* means *the act of*.

Therefore, *instruction* means *the act of building on*. Can you see how *instruction* has come to mean *teaching* or *education?* What you learn is *built on* what you know. Remember that the stem *struct* means *to build* or *building*. It will help you to get the meaning of many words that use *struct*.

To Do: Match the meaning in column B to the proper *struct* word in column A.

A	B
1. *instruction* in flying	(a) putting together
	(b) the act of teaching
2. *construct* the skyscraper	(c) the act of spoiling
	(d) a building
3. a tall *structure*	(e) build
4. bridge *construction*	
5. *destruction* of war	

A Little Harder: In column A there are five *struct* words with underlined prefixes or suffixes that you should know. Match the meaning in column B to the proper *struct* word in column A.

A	B
1. instruct<u>or</u>	(a) to build again
2. construct<u>ed</u>	(b) a person who teaches
3. structur<u>al</u>	(c) to teach again
4. <u>re</u>construct	(d) having to do with a structure
5. <u>re</u>instruct	(e) built (past tense)

EXPRESSING YOURSELF

1. Tell why you would or would not want to study about aviation if such a course were offered in your school.

27

2. The following people were famous pilots because they made flights that set records. Find out about one of them in an encyclopedia and tell why you would have enjoyed being with him (or her) on one of his (her) famous flights.

Charles Lindbergh   Amelia Earhart
Admiral Richard E. Byrd Ruth Nichols
Howard Hughes   Mrs. Betty Miller

3. Use an encyclopedia article on "Aviation" to find the answers to three of the following questions:

(a) What are some of the things an airline pilot must do before taking off?

(b) Who made the first round-the-world flight?

(c) What was the fastest speed ever flown by a pilot of a land plane?

(d) Who made the first flight across the Pacific Ocean?

(e) What is the longest distance flown in the air without refueling?

4. Tell in paragraph form of some other course you would like to see taught in your school.

5. SINKHOLES

YOU ARE DRIVING ALONG AND THE CAR IN FRONT OF YOU SUDDENLY SINKS INTO THE EARTH, OUT OF SIGHT.

HOW WOULD YOU EXPLAIN IT?

LAKELAND, Fla., April 29—Two cars dropped from sight, plunging to the bottom of a 30-foot sinkhole that turned up so *suddenly* the drivers could not avoid it.

No one was hurt, but the *incident* was the fifteenth of its kind reported in this area so far this year.

At a town 13 miles from Lakeland, two bedrooms of one house dropped into a hole 60 feet across and 35 feet deep. Part of the next house hung dangerously over the hole. The people in both houses had to be taken to safety.

Sinkholes have been happening without *warning* in this part of Florida for years. So far there is no way to *predict* when or where one will turn up. But when one does, others usually follow in the same area, usually along a straight line.

The worst sinkhole in *recent* years appeared in 1965. It was 70 feet across and 150 feet deep. It destroyed one house, *damaged* several others and cracked walls a city block away.

One hole, 15 feet deep, opened up this year in the middle of U.S. Highway 19 seconds after a car had driven by. Others in the same area occurred at night, damaging houses, swallowing up lawns, trees and parts of streets and causing 23 *frightened residents* to run away from their homes in nightclothes.

Sinkholes happen when the weather is very dry. The earth at the surface begins to drop into these cavities, like sand falling into a giant hourglass. A sinkhole results.

—NEW YORK TIMES

CHECK YOUR UNDERSTANDING

1. The main idea of this article is:
   (a) Sinkholes happen suddenly.

(b) Sinkholes have caused a great deal of destruction in Lakeland, Florida.

(c) Sinkholes are difficult to climb out of.

(d) Sinkholes only damage large houses.

2. In the accident described at the beginning of the story

(a) no one was hurt.

(b) five people were hurt.

(c) two houses fell into holes.

(d) the drivers were able to avoid the sinkhole.

3. Sinkholes can happen

(a) near houses.

(b) on highways.

(c) in small cities.

(d) anywhere.

4. The worst sinkhole that ever happened was

(a) 35 feet deep and 60 feet wide.

(b) 45 feet deep and 70 feet wide.

(c) 250 feet deep and 60 feet wide.

(d) 150 feet deep and 70 feet wide.

5. The number of sinkholes that have occurred in the area of Lakeland this year is

(a) 15.

(b) 30.

(c) 10.

(d) 35.

REACHING OUT

1. Sinkholes do *not* happen

(a) after a rainstorm.

(b) in a straight line.

(c) when the weather is very dry.

(d) where there are large holes beneath the ground.
2. Sinkholes occur because
   (a) there are large spaces under houses.
   (b) dry earth shifts and fills underground holes.
   (c) wet earth sucks in heavy things such as cars and houses.
   (d) Lakeland has an underground lake.

GETTING THE PICTURE

The good reader sees in his imagination the things that happen in the story he is reading. How good is your imagination? Pick out the words in the second column that will finish the picture started in the first column. The correct answer for the first one is (d), "Two cars plunged to the bottom of a 30-foot-deep sinkhole."

A	B
1. Two cars	(a) have swallowed up lawns, trees, and parts of streets.
2. Part of a house	(b) drops like sand falling into a giant hourglass.
3. Sinkholes	(c) ran away from their homes in nightclothes.
4. Frightened residents	(d) plunged to the bottom of a 30-foot-deep sinkhole.

5. The soil at the surface	(e) disappeared into a hole.

IMPROVING YOUR VOCABULARY

In the first column below are the ten words in italics from the story. Pick out the best "story" meaning for each of these words.

1. *suddenly* turned   (a) quickly; (b) early; (c) lately

2. the first *incident*   (a) moment; (b) number; (c) happening

3. happen without *warning*   (a) knowing afterward; (b) knowing before; (c) yelling loudly

4. *predict* the future   (a) to tell before; (b) to tell after; (c) to write

5. *recent* years   (a) not long ago; (b) a long time ago; (c) in the future

6. *damaged* the car   (a) worked; (b) drove; (c) spoiled

7. *frightened* the animals   (a) hurt; (b) scared; (c) angered

8. *residents* of the house   (a) people that live in a place; (b) people that work there; (c) people that are sick

9. *contains* a gift   (a) goes on; (b) has in itself; (c) gives

10. *cavities* in the ground   (a) bad teeth; (b) hiding places; (c) holes

WORD BUILDING

The word *contains* is used in the story above. It means *holds within limits.*

Contains is built up from two word parts: *con* is a prefix which means *together,* while *tain* is a stem which means *hold. Contains* therefore means *holds together.* Can you see how *contains* has come to mean *holds within limits?*

Usually, when you see *tain* in a word, it has the meaning of *hold.* The word part *ten* also often means *to hold.*

Examples: The word *maintain* means *to hold,* or *keep up.*

A *tenet* is *a belief someone holds.*

To Do: Match the word in column B to the proper *tain* word in column A.

A	B
1. *detain* the train	(a) amuse; have as a guest
2. *entertain* friends	
3. *sustain* your good work	(b) hold back; delay
	(c) keep; continue to own or use
4. *retain* a worker	
5. *obtain* a new car	(d) get hold of
	(e) keep up

A Little Harder: Match the word in column B to the proper *ten* word in column A.

A	B
1. *tenant* on the first floor	(a) keeping in custody; holding back

2. *tenacious* effort
3. *detention* after school
4. *maintenance* of a house
5. *retention* of what you learned

(b) keeping up in good condition
(c) person who pays rent to occupy a building
(d) a keeping in possession or use
(e) firm; stubborn

EXPRESSING YOURSELF

1. If your home were in an area that suddenly developed sinkholes, would you move? Why?
2. You are babysitting. The children want to hear a scary, spooky story. You begin, "As I fell through the sinkhole . . ." Continue the story.
3. In a paragraph, tell about a moment when you were faced with sudden danger.

Continued on Page 24, Col.

REVIEW OF LESSONS 1-5

IMPROVING YOUR VOCABULARY

It's time to stop and review the most important words from the first five stories. Choose the correct meaning for each of the words in the first column. (The number in parentheses after each word tells you the number of the story in which the word first appeared.)

1. actually (3) (a) in fact; (b) for the most part; (c) impossibly

2. adopted (2) (a) complained; (b) taken for one's own; (c) spoke about

3. aisle (2) (a) body of land surrounded by water; (b) passage between rows of seats; (c) air travel

36

4. arrival (4)   (a) roundabout way; (b) happening; (c) coming

5. aviation (4)   (a) science of flying airplanes; (b) practical learning; (c) a person who steers

6. brunette (2)   (a) a person with dark brown or black hair; (b) a very attractive person; (c) a person who lives in a particular place

7. brief (1)   (a) strange; (b) healthful; (c) short

8. cavities (5)   (a) teeth; (b) practices; (c) holes

9. celebrate (2)   (a) enjoy a special occasion; (b) think deeply about; (c) tell in advance

10. commented (2)   (a) said; (b) said on the radio; (c) spoke angrily

11. competed (2)   (a) caring only for oneself; (b) scared; (c) took part in a contest

12. contains (5)   (a) presents to another; (b) has in itself; (c) holds back

13. curb (3)   (a) talk over; (b) hold back; (c) like better

14. damaged (5)   (a) made very wet; (b) spoiled; (c) scared

15. detour (4)   (a) something in which to make a fire; (b) study of; (c) roundabout way

16. discuss (4)   (a) feel bad about; (b) cut from end to end; (c) talk over

17. eerie (1)   (a) necessary; (b) admitting air; (c) strange

18. exploding (1)   (a) telling the reasons for; (b) blowing up; (c) making a whirring sound

19. flight (4)   (a) air travel; (b) take part in a contest; (c) how high or low a sound is

20. frightened (5)   (a) scared; (b) spoiled; (c) appeared suddenly

21. furnace (1)   (a) present; (b) something in which to make a fire; (c) a train engine

22. generally (3)   (a) rarely; (b) for the most part; (c) always

23. habits (3)   (a) holes; (b) happenings; (c) practices

24. impossible (1)   (a) easily done; (b) not likely to happen; (c) not able to be done

25. incident (5)   (a) happening; (b) a dangerous event; (c) a happy occasion

26. instruction (4)   (a) entering the army; (b) breaking down; (c) teaching

27. locomotive (1)   (a) an engineer; (b) a train engine; (c) anything which goes fast

28. majority (3)   (a) more than half; (b) less than half; (c) more than anybody else

29. offer (4)   (a) to hope; (b) to wait for; (c) to present

30. permanent (4)   (a) beautiful; (b) not

able to be done; (c) lasting

31. pilot (4)   (a) a person who steers; (b) a person who lives in a place; (c) a person who makes plans

32. pitched (1)   (a) how high or low a sound is; (b) cut up and put together; (c) threw into a shallow hole

33. predict (5)   (a) get ready; (b) tell before; (c) enjoy a special occasion

34. preferred (3)   (a) took for one's own; (b) said; (c) liked more

35. recent (5)   (a) old; (b) not long ago; (c) strange

36. remarked (2)   (a) spoke; (b) did over; (c) brought together again

37. residents (5)   (a) doctors; (b) people who live in a certain place; (c) people in charge of a group or country

38. roared (1)   (a) whistled shrilly; (b) made a loud, deep noise; (c) spoiled

39. searched (2)   (a) found; (b) talked about; (c) looked for

40. snacks (3)   (a) healthful food; (b) light meals; (c) blows struck with an open hand

41. soaked (1)   (a) trapped; (b) looked for; (c) made very wet

42. split (1)
(a) brought together again; (b) cut from end to end; (c) tried very hard

43. stunning (2)
(a) very attractive; (b) healthy; (c) necessary

44. suddenly (5)
(a) quickly; (b) after a while; (c) for the most part

45. survey (3)
(a) teaching; (b) a study; (c) roundabout way

46. training (4)
(a) practical learning; (b) blowing up; (c) air travel

47. united (2)
(a) took apart; (b) took part in a contest; (c) brought together

48. vital (3)
(a) necessary; (b) not useful; (c) short

49. warning (5)
(a) heating up; (b) telling of danger before it happens; (c) coming soon

50. wholesome (3)
(a) full of holes; (b) not likely to happen; (c) healthful

WORD BUILDING

I. Match the word in column B to the proper word-building part in column A.

A	B
1. *ex* (1)	(a) build
2. *pre* (3)	(b) one

3. *struct* (4)   (c) out
4. *tain* (5)   (d) hold
5. *uni* (2)   (e) before

II. Choose the correct meaning for each of the words in the first column.

1. construct (4)   (a) build; (b) break down; (c) keep

2. construction (4) (a) putting together; (b) spoiling; (c) trying

3. destruction (4)   (a) putting together; (b) evening out; (c) spoiling

4. detain (5)   (a) be lively; (b) move; (c) hold back

5. entertain (5)   (a) have as a guest; (b) change; (c) enter rapidly

6. except (1)   (a) take in; (b) present; (c) leaving out

7. exchange (1)   (a) reason; (b) change from one to another; (c) keep

8. excited (1)   (a) left; (b) tried again; (c) stirred up

9. explained (1)   (a) described; (b) made fun of; (c) fought

10. exports (1)   (a) sends out; (b) sends back; (c) sends again

11. instruction (4) (a) putting away; (b) teaching; (c) insulting

12. obtain (5)   (a) reach for; (b) get hold of; (c) bring

13. retain (5)   (a) move again; (b) ask; (c) keep

14. structure (4)   (a) a rule; (b) a building; (c) a part of a whole

15. sustain (5)	(a) sign; (b) agree to; (c) keep up
16. uniform (2)	(a) of the same quality; (b) different; (c) heavy
17. union (2)	(a) a job; (b) a schedule; (c) a joining together
18. unit (2)	(a) open; (b) one part of a whole; (c) a space
19. unite (2)	(a) untie; (b) bring together; (c) leave out
20. united (2)	(a) a country; (b) made into one; (c) rebelled against

A Little Harder: Match the meaning in column B to the proper word in column A.

A	**B**
1. detention (5)	(a) person who pays rent to occupy space in a building
2. exclude (1)	
3. expose (1)	
4. maintenance (5)	(b) leave out
5. precaution (3)	(c) as one voice, in complete agreement
6. predict (3)	
7. preface (3)	(d) keeping in custody, holding back
8. tenant (5)	
9. unanimous (2)	(e) the introduction or part of the book that comes first
10. unique (2)	
	(f) tell before it happens
	(g) put into view
	(h) keeping up in good condition
	(i) care taken before
	(j) only one of its kind

6. TURKISH TOWN TALKS IN WHISTLES

WHY WOULD PEOPLE COMMUNICATE WITH EACH OTHER WITHOUT USING WORDS?

WHY MIGHT WHISTLING BE USED IN PLACE OF LANGUAGE?

In the *remote* Turkish village of Kuskoy, whistling is as important as talking. In fact, whistling is talking because the villagers speak and sing in whistles. Kuskoy parents begin to teach their boys and girls the language of whistling about the time the children learn to talk. It is *considered* so important that the village schoolmaster *includes* it as one of the subjects taught along with the Turkish language.

This art of *communication* has *developed* through the *centuries*. The village of Kuskoy spreads out across two hillsides that are separated by a deep valley. The villagers had to find an easy way to communicate where their voices couldn't carry. They developed a high-pitched whistle that could be heard for five miles. As a result, Kuskoy, which means "bird village" in Turkish, has come to be known as a whistler's *paradise*.

The whistler forms his "speech" with the tongue curled around his teeth so that the "words" are forced through lips that are not rounded in the usual whistling style; they are stretched flat across the face. The palm of the left hand is cupped about the mouth, and air is forced from the lungs. To someone who has not heard the sound before, it is like the *terrifying* whistle of a steam locomotive.

Whistling is so much a part of everyday life here that men and women speak, disagree and make love in whistles. A village wise man recently told the story of a young couple that *eloped*. The news was sent over the "mountain telephone" whistle. The lovers' adventure was quickly known. At weddings, the Kuskoy whistle becomes more musical. Kuskoyans "sing" to the *melody* played on the kemenche, a string instrument.

It is little wonder, then, that the children of

Kuskoy study whistling in school. Wouldn't it be great fun to start the class day with the school song —whistled of course!

—NEW YORK TIMES

CHECK YOUR UNDERSTANDING

1. Another title that would best explain the main idea of this story is:
   (a) Learn to Whistle at an Early Age
   (b) Turkish Villagers Whistle to Communicate
   (c) Whistling Is Fun
   (d) The Turkish Language
2. The whistler forms his high-pitched whistle by
   (a) cupping his hands around his mouth.
   (b) forcing air from his lungs.
   (c) blowing a locomotive whistle.
   (d) rounding his lips in the usual way.
3. The children of Kuskoy learn to whistle because
   (a) it is fun.
   (b) it is an important way to communicate.
   (c) it helps them to learn singing.
   (d) it is like the Turkish language.
4. In Kuskoy, whistling as a method of communication started
   (a) recently.
   (b) hundreds of years ago.
   (c) fifty years ago.
   (d) ten years ago.
5. The high-pitched whistle can be heard for a distance of
   (a) ten miles.
   (b) fifty miles.
   (c) one hundred miles.
   (d) five miles.

REACHING OUT

1. Whistling is *not*
   (a) used for speaking.
   (b) used by the children.
   (c) taught in the school.
   (d) used in place of Turkish.
2. The geography of Kuskoy could best be described as
   (a) a jungle.
   (b) hilly country.
   (c) a desert.
   (d) below sea level.

PUTTING THE PIECES TOGETHER

Titles for each of the five paragraphs in the story are listed below. Put these titles in the same order as the paragraphs in the story.

1. Whistling at Weddings
2. Whistling the School Song
3. Why Whistling Is Important in Kuskoy
4. How Whistling Developed in Kuskoy
5. How a Kuskoy Villager Whistles

IMPROVING YOUR VOCABULARY

In the first column below are the ten words in italics from the story. Pick out the best "story" meaning for each of these words.

1. a *remote* village   (a) far-off; (b) musical; (c) foreign

2. *considered* important   (a) thought to be; (b) made to be; (c) tried out as

3. *includes* it as a school subject   (a) keeps away from; (b) puts in; (c) decides on

4. art of *communication*   (a) whistling; (b) giving information; (c) being important

5. *developed* with time   (a) went away; (b) was talked about; (c) grew

6. through the *centuries*   (a) periods of 100 years; (b) villages located in valleys; (c) rulers of Turkey

7. whistler's *paradise*   (a) school; (b) heaven; (c) parade

8. *terrifying* whistle   (a) very frightening; (b) beautiful; (c) low-pitched

9. couple *eloped*   (a) talked in whistles; (b) had an argument; (c) ran away to get married

10. played a *melody*   (a) poem; (b) rhythm; (c) tune

WORD BUILDING

The word *adventure* is used in the story above. It means *an unusual and exciting experience.*

Adventure is built up from two important word parts: *ad* is a prefix which means *to,* and *ven* is a stem which means *come. Adventure* means *coming to* something unusual.

Usually, when you see *ven* in a word, it means *come*.

Example: An *avenue* is a way of *coming* to a place.

To Do: Match the word in column B to the proper *ven* word in column A.

A	B
1. political *convention*	(a) a happening
2. exciting *event*	(b) a meeting
3. *invent* a better mousetrap	(c) keep from happening
4. *prevent* an accident	(d) handy; easy to use or get to
5. *convenient* place to meet	(e) think up; produce something new

A Little Harder: Match, as above.

A	B
1. a way of getting *revenue*	(a) finally
2. *intervene* in a fight	(b) income
3. a *souvenir* of the trip	(c) come between
4. a game *eventually* won	(d) something kept as a reminder
5. a business *venture*	(e) a risky undertaking

EXPRESSING YOURSELF

1. Make believe that you are teaching someone how to whistle. How would you describe the process to him?

2. How do you or your friends use the whistle to communicate?

3. Smoke signals are another form of communication. Tell about three other ways in which people can "talk" to each other without using words.

4. Try to communicate with another student in your class by whistling to him.

5. It makes sense for the children of the Turkish village to study whistling in school. What suggestions do you have for practical subjects which you would like to study during the regular school day?

6. The Kuskoy whistle sounds "like the terrifying whistle of a steam locomotive." Here, the author tried to help you hear the sound by comparing it to another sound you are probably familiar with. The good writer uses striking comparisons. See if you can make up a striking comparison for each of these sounds:

   (a) a kettle boiling
   (b) rain on a window.
   (c) a baseball hitting against a bat
   (d) the school cafeteria
   (e) bowling pins falling
   (f) the crowd at a football game when the home team scores a touchdown

7. DROP-OUT VETERAN GETS DIPLOMA

IS IT REALLY SO IMPORTANT TO FINISH HIGH SCHOOL?

WHY?

The day after Tom Oliver dropped out of East High School, he knew he had made a mistake. But he had *differed* so with the principal that he was too *embarrassed* to go back. He went downtown to the *adult* high school, but he dropped out of that, too, after only a few months. "I don't know—I guess I couldn't *adjust,*" he explained.

Now, four years later, Oliver—a twice-wounded Vietnam war *veteran*—is scheduled to get his *diploma* in the adult high school's graduation Wednesday night.

"I thought I'd feel different because I'm not graduating with my high school class," he said. "But I don't. I'm so darned glad to be getting it."

Glad to Be Alive

Actually, Tom Oliver is glad to be alive.

Early one February morning last year, he and the rest of his squad walked into enemy fire. "We were coming off an all-night patrol," he said. "We walked right into an enemy trap."

Six in the squad were killed. Eight others were wounded. Oliver was hit first by *fragments* from a small bomb. Then he was hit with machine-gun and rifle fire. His right shoulder, left arm, and left hip were broken.

As he and his buddies lay wounded, enemy soldiers rushed out and grabbed their weapons, thinking all the GI's were dead.

After more than five months in hospitals, Oliver was *discharged* from the army last July.

Arriving Home

One of the first things Oliver did when he *arrived* in Los Angeles after a tiring trip back from Southeast Asia was to go into an airport waiting room to get a beer.

51

Oliver, a Negro who feels strongly that he fought for his country as well as any white American, told about what happened to him in this way:

"I was *determined* to get waited on. So I waited and waited while everyone around was served. It took about 45 minutes to get the beer. By then I needed one."

He also ran into great *difficulty* finding an apartment in Milwaukee.

Plans

Oliver plans to enter college next fall. He said he might play football. His brother is a former college football player and is now a teacher at a Milwaukee junior high school.

Oliver said he might want to study social work in college. "But I'm not 100% sure," he added.

Why social work?

Oliver replied that he thought he might be able to help the youngsters in the juvenile detention home.

"I was there once," he said. "The thought of it is always with me."

—MILWAUKEE JOURNAL

CHECK YOUR UNDERSTANDING

1. Another title that would best explain the main idea of this story is:
   (a) Tom Oliver, Lucky Veteran
   (b) Twice Wounded

(c) How to Stay Alive

(d) Becoming a Social Worker

2. Tom Oliver dropped out of school because
   (a) he was expelled by the principal.
   (b) he was too embarrassed to return after his quarrel with his principal.
   (c) he felt that he couldn't do the work.
   (d) he wanted to go to Vietnam.

3. After the enemy attacked, Tom's squad
   (a) was wiped out.
   (b) lost six men.
   (c) killed the enemy.
   (d) saved its leader.

4. In college, Tom may major in
   (a) football.
   (b) social work.
   (c) English.
   (d) education.

5. Tom had difficulty finding an apartment because
   (a) there were few available.
   (b) he was a Negro.
   (c) he was sick.
   (d) the rents were very high.

REACHING OUT

1. Tom Oliver did *not*
   (a) finish his high school education.
   (b) get wounded in Vietnam.
   (c) wait 45 minutes for a beer.
   (d) enter college when this story was written.

2. The word that best describes Tom's action when he waited for a drink is
(a) happy.
(b) friendly.
(c) determined.
(d) impatient.

ORGANIZING EFFECTIVELY

This story is divided into four parts:
A. Finishing High School
B. Glad to Be Alive
C. Arriving Home
D. Plans

Here are ten details from the story. Under which of the above topics would you expect to find each of these facts? Write the letter of the topic next to the fact. The first one is done for you.

1. wounds   B   (Glad to Be Alive)
2. a diploma
3. a squad
4. a beer
5. a bomb
6. a difference with the principal
7. a juvenile detention home
8. a football player
9. an apartment
10. going to college

FIRST THINGS FIRST

Arrange these events in the order in which they happened.

1. Tom is scheduled to get his diploma from adult evening high school.
2. Tom was hit by fragments from a mine.
3. Tom was discharged from the hospital after five months.
4. Tom's buddies were wounded.
5. Tom waited to be served some beer.
6. Tom lived in a juvenile home.
7. Tom had difficulty getting an apartment.
8. Tom may want to study social work in college.

IMPROVING YOUR VOCABULARY

In the first column below are the ten words in italics from the story. Pick out the best "story" meaning for each of these words.

1. *differed* with the principal — (a) disagreed; (b) a talk; (c) an understanding
2. too *embarrassed* to return — (a) angry; (b) smart; (c) ashamed
3. *adult* high school — (a) for grown-up persons; (b) for dropouts; (c) co-educational
4. couldn't *adjust* — (a) do one's work; (b) fit; (c) explain one's feelings
5. war *veteran* — (a) a person who has served in the armed forces; (b) hero; (c) draftee
6. got his *diploma* — (a) discharge from the armed forces; (b) certificate of skill or ability at

		a trade; (c) certificate given by a school at graduation
7.	bomb *fragments*	(a) bullets; (b) pieces broken off; (c) small explosions
8.	*discharged* from the army	(a) let go; (b) enlisted; (c) given a medal
9.	*determined* to get waited on	(a) firmly decided on; (b) waited patiently; (c) next on line
10.	ran into *difficulty*	(a) friendship; (b) ease; (c) trouble

---

WORD BUILDING

The word *difficulty* is used in the story above. It means *something hard to do*.

Difficulty is built up from two important word parts: *dif,* or *dis,* is a prefix which means *not,* and *fic* is a stem which means *make,* or *do.* A *difficulty* is something you *can not easily do.*

Usually, when you see *fic* in a word, it means *make,* or *do.* Often, *fic* appears as *fac* or *fec.*

Example: *Manufacture* first meant to *make by hand.* Now it means *to make anything on a large scale, especially by machine.*

To Do: Match the word in column B to the proper *fac* word in column A.

A	**B**
1. a *factory* worker	(a) a person who helps another
2. a *fact*	

56

3. the boy's *benefactor*

4. a *factor* in winning the war

5. a member of the *faculty*

(b) all the teachers in a school

(c) a thing that has actually happened

(d) a condition that brings about a result

(e) a building where things are made

A Little Harder: Match the word in column B to the proper *fac, fec,* or *fic* word in column A.

A

1. *facsimile* of a magazine

2. no *facility* for swimming

3. *beneficial* for health

4. *ineffective* studying

5. *sufficient* food

B

(a) not producing a desired result

(b) an exact copy

(c) a means by which something can easily be done

(d) leading to good

(e) enough; as much as is needed

EXPRESSING YOURSELF

1. Statistics show that high school graduates can earn more money than dropouts. Why else would someone want to get a high school diploma?

2. Tell about a serious mistake that you made, and what you did to try to correct it.

3. On his return to the United States, Tom Oliver experienced racial prejudice, after having twice been wounded fighting for his country. What would you have done if you had been Tom Oliver waiting to be served?

4. Imagine that you are Tom answering a letter from a friend back in the United States who has written you saying he is planning to drop out of high school. Write Tom's letter.

8. BLIND BOWLER

IS BLINDNESS THE WORST THING THAT CAN HAPPEN TO A PERSON?

HOW DID JOE FEINBERG ADJUST TO BEING BLIND?

Many of the bowlers left their alleys in the middle of games and lined up three and four deep to watch a short, barrel-chested, 53-year-old man take four steps and swiftly roll a bowling ball. The crowd was plainly surprised at the speed and *accuracy* of the ball and broke into loud *applause* as the pins fell.

Joe Feinberg, who cannot see the pins fall because he is blind, hears each *ovation*. He claps his hands, does a little dance and smiles like a young bowler who has just rolled his first strike.

With over 50 *trophies* to his credit, Mr. Feinberg is one of the most famous blind bowlers in the United States.

In a National Blind Bowlers Tournament in Cincinnati, Mr. Feinberg's three-game series of 580 (184, 202, 194) was the highest score of the 700 bowlers competing in the *event*.

Mr. Feinberg bowls more than 20 games a day at any one of 20 Brooklyn lanes to which he has a standing invitation. His way of bowling is unusual among the blind.

Almost all blind bowlers use a rail that leads them along the *approach* to the alley. Mr. Feinberg uses nothing at all. He stands against the *circular* table upon which the balls return. A sighted person tells him how many pins are left on the alley and their positions. Then Mr. Feinberg lines up his approach by stepping to one of the five dots that are at the back of the bowling alley for the *guidance* of all bowlers. He uses a different dot for different bowling *situations*.

Mr. Feinberg is a *former* master electrician who lost his sight in an accident seven years ago. For the first three years of his blindness he hardly left the apartment he shares with his wife. He worried about his loss of sight.

Then, he explained, "I went to the Industrial Home for the Blind and learned of people being trained there as experts in electrical wiring. I wondered why I couldn't bowl, why I couldn't walk 15 feet, roll a ball and walk back 15 feet. I tried.

"I used to bowl before I was blind," he recalled. "But I wasn't very good because I used to watch all the pretty girls passing by. Now all I have is a picture of the pins in my mind."

—NEW YORK TIMES

CHECK YOUR UNDERSTANDING

1. Another title that would best explain the main idea of this story is:
   (a) How to Bowl
   (b) Overcoming a Handicap
   (c) The Industrial Home for the Blind
   (d) Taking Care of Your Health
2. Joe Feinberg
   (a) bowls like all sighted bowlers.
   (b) uses the special bowling style of the blind.
   (c) bowls an average of 15 games a day.
   (d) uses sound to spot his pins.
3. Mr. Feinberg is able to make his spares by
   (a) starting on the third spot.
   (b) walking 15 feet to the right.
   (c) finding out their position from a sighted person.
   (d) using the pin-spotting machine.
4. Mr. Feinberg became blind
   (a) at birth.
   (b) before he started to bowl.
   (c) about seven years ago.
   (d) before he married.
5. Mr. Feinberg
   (a) does not bowl anymore.
   (b) bowls more since he became blind.
   (c) bowls less since he became blind.
   (d) began bowling by accident.

REACHING OUT

1. Mr. Feinberg did *not* want to
   - (a) bowl for seven years.
   - (b) leave his apartment for three years.
   - (c) enter a bowling tournament.
   - (d) change his bowling style.
2. Most likely, Mr. Feinberg took up bowling again because
   - (a) it was easy.
   - (b) an owner of a bowling alley started him.
   - (c) he was encouraged by what other blind people learned.
   - (d) his wife suggested it.
3. Mr. Feinberg does *not*
   - (a) use a hand rail to bowl.
   - (b) start from the circular return table.
   - (c) use dots to line up a shot.
   - (d) get help to make spares.

FIRST THINGS FIRST

Arrange these events in the order in which they happened.
1. Joe Feinberg learned to bowl differently than other blind people.
2. For the first three years after his blindness Joe Feinberg did nothing.
3. Joe Feinberg lost his sight in an accident.
4. Joe Feinberg won over 50 trophies.
5. Joe Feinberg wanted to learn to bowl after he visited the Industrial Home for the Blind.

GETTING THE PICTURE

The good reader sees in his imagination the things that happen in the story he is reading. You cannot fully appreciate this story unless you see exactly what is happening as Joe Feinberg, a blind bowler, prepares to bowl.

A	**B**
1. Joe Feinberg stood on the same spot	(a) as he lined up his approach for a spare.
2. Joe Feinberg clapped his hands	(b) as his ball was being returned.
3. Joe Feinberg waited by the circular table	(c) as he heard the applause from the crowd.
4. Joe Feinberg talked to a man	(d) as he prepared to throw his first ball.
5. Joe Feinberg carefully selected a spot in the back of the alley	(e) as he got a picture in his mind of the pins left standing.

IMPROVING YOUR VOCABULARY

In the first column below are the ten words in italics from the story. Pick out the best "story" meaning for each of these words.

1. bowled with *accuracy*   (a) exactness; (b) force; (c) beauty

2. loud *applause*   (a) approval shown by handclapping, cheering,

etc.; (b) booing and jeering; (c) cries of discontent

3. hears each *ovation*   (a) fall; (b) month; (c) cheering

4. won 50 *trophies*   (a) prizes; (b) bowling balls; (c) alleys

5. competing in the *event*   (a) score; (b) tie game; (c) sports contest

6. *approach* to the alley   (a) side rail; (b) first line; (c) the way by which a place can be reached

7. *circular* table   (a) square; (b) round; (c) large

8. lines for *guidance*   (a) scorekeeping; (b) direction; (c) use

9. different *situations*   (a) rights; (b) games; (c) positions

10. *former* electrician   (a) past; (b) agricultural worker; (c) excellent

---

WORD BUILDING

The word *position* is used in the story above. It means *place.*

Position is built up from the stem *pos* which means *put,* or *place.*

Usually, when you see *pos* in a word, it means *put,* or *place.* Often, *pos* may appear as *pon.*

Example: A *deposit* is a *putting down.* When you deposit money in a bank, you place it there for safekeeping.

To Do: Match the word in column B to the proper *pos* word in column A.

A	**B**
1. *expose* the truth	(a) imagine; think to be
2. *suppose* he will be	true
there	(b) completely different
3. *opposite* to his	(c) certain; sure
brother	(d) rest
4. *positive* he is right	(e) show; make known
5. state of *repose*	

A Little Harder: Match the word in column B to the proper *pos* or *pon* word in column A.

A	**B**
1. radio *component*	(a) remove from office
2. *postpone* the game	(b) one who is against
3. *opponent* in the	you
contest	(c) put off for later;
4. *depose* the king	delay
5. *impose* his will on	(d) force on others
the group	(e) a part

EXPRESSING YOURSELF

1. Tell about people you have known who have had some physical handicap; how well have they managed in spite of their handicap?
2. Describe in a paragraph what might happen if you tried to bowl the way Joe Feinberg does.
3. For whom do you think blindness is a worse experience: a person born blind or a teen-ager who loses his sight? Why?
4. Handicapped people are sensitive about their problem. Make up a list of five rules you think people should follow in dealing with handicapped people.

9. RESCUE BY HUMAN CHAIN

38 CHILDREN AND 9 ADULTS FACED DEATH BY DROWNING.

HOW DID QUICK THINKING SAVE THEIR LIVES?

NEW YORK CITY—A human chain rescued 38 frightened kindergarten children from their school bus which had *stalled* in a *flooded* underpass in Central Park.

The 9 adults who were also aboard *escaped* safely after they pushed the children, some screaming in fear, through windows to the *clutching* hands of the line of rescuers. Minutes after the rescue was finished, the water, which was rushing out of a nearby broken main, completely covered the bus.

There were moments of *panic* in the bus among the children. The 8 teachers aboard tried to *calm* them. The water rose swiftly up the sides of the bus as 3 policemen struggled in the *rapidly* rising water to begin the human chain.

Sergeant Richard Mason and 2 other police officers stripped off their gunbelts, coats and shoes and waded in. The water was already waist high. They could *scarcely* stand up as thousands of gallons of water raced into the underpass.

"I yelled to the driver not to open the door but to start handing the children out of the window," Mason said later. "The water was flowing like a mountain stream and I feared if he opened the door some kids would get pulled right out into it. It was a *miracle* that no one was hurt."

The 3 policemen were waist deep when they passed the first 3 children to safety. "Then suddenly we were up to our armpits," Mason said. "I called for help to Park Department men who were arriving, and other police, too. Everyone knew the danger. We would have lost some of those kids if we had wasted any time."

Mason said the human chain grew to about 13 officers and park men spaced about an arm's length apart. "We had to do it fast. We sort of threw each child to the next man in line. As we yelled for more help some of the kids started screaming. There was some panic. By the time the last child was out, the water was above the seats and about up to window level."

Meanwhile, aboard the bus, Mrs. Arlene Lewis, one of the 8 teachers, was trying to help keep order. "We were standing on the seats. It was *incredible,*" she said. "When I got out myself and stood there and watched the water come right up over that bus, I'll tell you, I knew then what a close call we had had."

—NEWSDAY, LONG ISLAND, N.Y.

CHECK YOUR UNDERSTANDING

1. Another title that would best explain the main idea of this story is:
   (a) Chains
   (b) One Rainy Day
   (c) A Close Call
   (d) A Bus Ride
2. The children in the bus
   (a) showed no fear.
   (b) swam to safety.
   (c) calmed their teachers.
   (d) were frightened.
3. The number of people in the human chain outside the bus grew to about
   (a) 38.
   (b) 3.
   (c) 9.
   (d) 13.
4. When the children started to scream
   (a) the adults on the bus tried to calm them.
   (b) the bus driver stopped the bus.

(c) some of the adults began to scream, too.

(d) the policemen stopped passing them out to the other rescuers.

FIRST THINGS FIRST

Arrange these events in the order in which they happened.

1. Sergeant Mason yelled to the driver not to open the door.
2. The bus stalled in the underpass.
3. All the children were rescued.
4. A water main broke near the underpass.
5. The 9 adults escaped safely.
6. Water completely covered the bus.
7. The 3 policemen passed the first 3 children to safety.

WHAT'S THE REASON?

Good readers are good detectives. They see *why* things happen. See if you can find the proper *why* to complete each statement.

1. The children were screaming because
    (a) they were frightened.
    (b) they were having fun.
    (c) they were angry at the bus driver.
    (d) they wanted to open the door of the bus.
2. Sergeant Mason told the driver not to open the door because
    (a) he wanted the driver to keep the bus moving.

(b) he was afraid some of the children would be pulled into the rising water.

(c) he thought the driver was trying to run out.

(d) he wanted to climb in through the window.

3. The human chain was made
   (a) to make the children think it was all a game.
   (b) to pass the children to safety.
   (c) to give the men courage to carry on.
   (d) to help get the bus started again.

4. It was important to work quickly because
   (a) it was getting dark.
   (b) the children were afraid.
   (c) some of the Park Department men had to get back to their jobs.
   (d) the water kept rising.

5. No one was hurt because
   (a) none of the children became afraid.
   (b) the water finally stopped rising.
   (c) the teachers were strong swimmers.
   (d) a number of people worked together to help.

GETTING THE PICTURE

The good reader sees in his imagination the things that happen in the story he is reading. You cannot fully appreciate this story unless you see exactly what is happening as the water moves from one level to another.

Pick out the words in column B that will correctly finish the picture of the rising water level in column A.

	A		**B**
1.	The water was waist high	(a)	as the last child was pulled out.
2.	The water was up to the policemen's armpits	(b)	when the policemen waded in.
3.	The water was above the seats, up to window level	(c)	a few minutes after the rescue.
4.	The water was completely over the bus	(d)	after the first three children were passed out of the bus.

IMPROVING YOUR VOCABULARY

In the first column below are the ten words in italics from the story. Pick out the best "story" meaning for each of these words.

1. *stalled* car — (a) went through water; (b) stopped against one's wishes; (c) be in an accident

2. *flooded* underpass — (a) filled with water; (b) dark; (c) long and winding

3. *escaped* safely — (a) got free; (b) jumped; (c) ran

4. *clutching* hands — (a) wet; (b) holding tight; (c) panicky

5. *panic* in the bus — (a) loss of self-control brought on by fear; (b) a time for fun; (c) fighting due to lack of adult attention

6. *calm* the children   (a) make speeches to; (b) make quiet; (c) strike
7. *rapidly* rising water   (a) slowly; (b) roughly; (c) swiftly
8. *scarcely* stand   (a) easily; (b) in a frightened way; (c) hardly
9. a *miracle* no one was hurt   (a) fact; (b) laughing matter; (c) a wonder
10. *incredible* event   (a) beautiful; (b) horrible; (c) unbelievable

---

WORD BUILDING

The word *incredible* is used in the story above. It means *unbelievable.*

Incredible is built up from the prefix *in* meaning *not,* the stem *cred* meaning *believe,* and the suffix *able.* The word therefore means *not able to be believed.*

Usually, when you see *cred* in a word, it means *believe,* or *trust.*

Example: The word *creed* means a statement of *belief.*

To Do: Match the word in column B to the proper *cred* word in column A.

A	**B**
1. bought food on *credit*	(a) believing too easily
2. showed his *credentials*	(b) trust
3. *discredit* his statement	(c) trustworthiness; believability
	(d) bring doubt on; disbelieve

72

4. a *credulous* young person

5. poor *credibility*

(e) letter or certificate showing one's right to a certain position

A Little Harder: Match, as above.

A	**B**
1. *incredulous* look on his face	(a) belief
2. gave little *credence* to his story	(b) a statement of belief
	(c) one to whom a debt is owed
3. *creditable* achievement	(d) showing doubt or disbelief
4. the *creditor* wants to collect	(e) bringing honor
5. my *credo*	

EXPRESSING YOURSELF

1. A reporter said, "Panic was a greater danger to the children than was the water." Explain that statement.

2. It has been said that a person could be dying on the street of a big city and no one would stop to help him. Tell of a real experience in which people did (or did not) come to the aid of someone who was in danger.

3. Imagine you were on the bus as the water kept rising. What would you do or say to the children to calm and reassure them?

4. Tell about a situation you were in where lack of cooperation brought about failure.

5. Imagine you are one of these people: the bus driver, the teacher (Mrs. Lewis), or the policeman (Sergeant Mason). In a paragraph, tell what happened to you during the incident described in this story. Or, as the bus driver, write out the complete report of the incident, which you will turn in to your company

10. GIRL IN A MAN'S WORLD

WOMEN DRIVERS! ARE THEY REALLY POORER DRIVERS THAN MEN?

HAS DIANA CARTER MADE A MISTAKE BY ENTERING A FIELD USUALLY RESERVED "FOR MEN ONLY"?

In high school in Toronto, Diana Elizabeth Carter spent more time in garages, waiting for her dates to fix their cars, than she did at dances or even in class.

Not one to sit around, Diana was soon helping the boys patch, repair and tune up their cars. But no matter how much she hinted, none of them would let her race their cars.

Then she went to work for *Track and Traffic,* Canada's only sports-car magazine. The boss thought she could become a racer and lent her his car for a 10-mile run for *novices.* Diana beat the other 24 drivers, all men, and won her first trophy.

The man who placed second came over to find out who beat him. When Diana removed her helmet he spluttered in *disgust:* "A girl!"

Diana now owns 50 trophies and is considered Canada's top lady auto racer. She has finished in the top five in over 100 races, mostly against men. There are, at most, 15 other women drivers in Canada, but they don't last for more than 2 seasons. Diana has been at it *steadily* for 7.

Slender and blonde, Diana is an only child. Her father, a *retired* engineer, keeps saying he's going to come out on the track and beat her.

"And he's 76," Diana says. "I think he's secretly *jealous.*"

Diana recalls the only accident she's had while racing. The rain was coming down in sheets; the track was slippery. She pushed the *accelerator* down to the floor while coming around a turn, then went into a spin. The car *toppled* end over end, landing upright against a fence, but Diana was unscratched. A few kids watched her hop out of the car and yelled: "Look! It's a girl."

"All I was thinking of was how much it would cost to repair the wreck," Diana says.

In 7 years of racing her total prize money comes to about $4,000. With entry *fees* and *trans-*

portation, even driving a low-priced car, it costs her about $6,000 a year to race.

In spite of the dangers of racing, she'd rather be on a track than a thruway. She knows what to expect on a track. On a thruway she has to do "defensive driving," figure out what the next driver, coming or going, will do.

"They may make a safe car soon," Diana says, "but there's no way they can make a safe driver in a hurry."

NEW YORK DAILY NEWS
("Only Human" by Sidney Fields)

CHECK YOUR UNDERSTANDING

1. Another title that would best explain the main idea of this story is:
   (a) Smashup
   (b) Auto-Racing Thrills
   (c) A Pretty Girl
   (d) Girl Auto Racer
2. Diana Carter is different from most girls because
   (a) she drives an automobile.
   (b) she has been in an automobile accident.
   (c) she comes from Canada.
   (d) she has won auto races.
3. Diana
   (a) has never lost a race.
   (b) is one of several children.
   (c) has won 50 trophies.
   (d) was once badly hurt in an accident.
4. According to this story, Diana spent most of her time as a high school girl

(a) at dances.
(b) in garages.
(c) in school.
(d) racing her boy friends' cars.

REACHING OUT

1. From the information in this story, we can conclude that Diana drives in auto races
   (a) to make money.
   (b) because she is jealous of her father.
   (c) because she enjoys it.
   (d) because she has to, in order to work for *Track and Traffic*.
2. "Defensive driving" means
   (a) thruway driving.
   (b) racetrack driving.
   (c) figuring out what other drivers on the road will do.
   (d) driving very rapidly.

PUTTING THE PIECES TOGETHER

The twelve paragraphs of this story can be broken down into seven main topics, or parts. Below is a title for each of these seven parts. Put these titles in the same order as the parts appear in the story.

1. Diana and Her Father
2. The Cost of Auto Racing
3. Diana in High School
4. Thruway Driving vs. Raceway Driving

5. Diana's First Race
6. Diana's Trophies and Record as a Driver
7. Diana's Only Accident

IMPROVING YOUR VOCABULARY

In the first column below are the ten words in italics from the story. Pick out the best "story" meaning for each of these words.

1. a run for *novices*   (a) experts; (b) drag racers; (c) beginners
2. spluttered in *disgust*   (a) surprise; (b) fear; (c) strong dislike
3. driving *steadily*   (a) happily; (b) regularly; (c) carelessly
4. a *slender* girl   (a) plump; (b) well-dressed; (c) slim
5. a *retired* engineer   (a) professional; (b) no longer working; (c) very old
6. secretly *jealous*   (a) wishing for something someone else has; (b) wanting to be young again; (c) fearful of something very bad happening
7. pushed down on the automobile's *accelerator*   (a) brake; (b) gas pedal; (c) steering wheel
8. *toppled* over   (a) skidded; (b) fell; (c) leaped up
9. entry *fees*   (a) money paid for services or privileges; (b) licenses for driving; (c)

opening races to eliminate poorer drivers

10. *transportation* costs — (a) automobile repair; (b) way of going from one place to another; (c) hospital care

---

WORD BUILDING

The word *transportation* is used in the story above. It means *a way of being carried from one place to another.*

Transportation is built up from two main word parts: *trans* is a prefix which means *across,* and *port* is a stem which means to *carry.* You can easily see how the word has come to have the meaning it has.

Usually, when you see *trans* at the start of a word, it has the meaning of *across.*

Example: *Transatlantic* means *across the Atlantic Ocean.*

To Do: Match the word in column B to the proper *trans* word in column A.

A	**B**
1. *transfer* to another job	(a) send out
2. *translate* from Spanish	(b) a small window just above a door
3. *transmit* the message	(c) change from one place to another
4. look through the *transom*	(d) able to be seen through
5. a *transparent* cover	(e) change from one language to another

A Little Harder: Match, as above.

A	B
1. *transform* the organization	(a) carry on business
2. lost in *transit*	(b) temporary
3. a *transitory* moment	(c) interchange
4. *transpose* the two figures	(d) change the form of
5. *transact* an agreement	(e) going from one place to another

---

EXPRESSING YOURSELF

1. Tell what you think about women drivers.
2. Interview a driver-education teacher. Ask him whether he finds it more difficult to teach boys or girls to drive.
3. Are there any occupations not suitable for women? Should a girl be able to enter every occupation? Explain your views.
4. Here is a quote from a letter to the editor of a newspaper: "Auto racing is a sport that is both daring and dangerous. It is a sport for men, not women." Write your own letter to the editor, agreeing or disagreeing with this quote.
5. In what sports can women compete against men? In what sports do you think women can never be men's equals?
6. Diana Carter feels that there is more danger on an express highway than there is in an auto race. In a paragraph, tell why you agree or disagree with her.

REVIEW OF LESSONS 6-10

IMPROVING YOUR VOCABULARY

Choose the correct meaning for each of the words in the first column. (The number in parentheses after each word tells you the number of the story where the word first appeared.)

1. accelerator (10)   (a) giving information; (b) certificate given by a school at graduation; (c) gas pedal

2. accuracy (8)   (a) exactness; (b) cheering; (c) fight with words

3. adjust (7)   (a) decide on; (b) let go; (c) fit

4. adult (7)   (a) wishing for something someone else has; (b) for grown-up persons; (c) a person who has served in the armed forces

5. applause (8) (a) a dessert; (b) heaven; (c) approval shown by handclapping or cheering

6. approach (8) (a) a piece broken off; (b) sports contest; (c) the way by which a place can be reached

7. calm (9) (a) thought about; (b) make quiet; (c) stop against one's wishes

8. centuries (6) (a) rulers of countries; (b) periods of 50 years; (c) periods of 100 years

9. circular (8) (a) round; (b) wonderful; (c) slim

10. clutching (9) (a) very frightening; (b) holding tight; (c) attempting

11. communication (6) (a) making noise; (b) giving information; (c) telling jokes

12. considered (6) (a) made; (b) thought to be; (c) wanted to be

13. determined (7) (a) firmly decided on; (b) let go; (c) stopped

14. developed (6) (a) grew; (b) grew smaller; (c) took photographs of

15. differed (7) (a) spoke; (b) disagreed; (c) consented

16. difficulty (7) (a) direction; (b) strong dislike; (c) trouble

17. diploma (7) (a) certificate given by a school at graduation; (b) money paid for services or privileges; (c) loud and long applause

18. discharged (7) (a) took up again; (b) let go; (c) fell forward

19. disgust (10) (a) fight with words; (b) loss of self-control brought on by fear; (c) strong dislike

20. eloped (6) (a) ran away to get married; (b) no longer worked; (c) fell down

21. embarrassed (7) (a) fell forward; (b) ashamed; (c) went far from

22. escaped (9) (a) got free; (b) stopped against one's wishes; (c) put in

23. event (8) (a) the way by which a place can be reached; (b) a sports contest; (c) a prize

24. fees (10) (a) money paid for services or privileges; (b) pieces broken off; (c) prizes

25. flooded (9) (a) stopped against one's wishes; (b) calmed; (c) filled with water

26. former (8) (a) far-off; (b) round; (c) past

27. fragments (7) (a) pieces broken off; (b) beginners; (c) positions

28. guidance (8) (a) a wonder; (b) cheering; (c) direction

29. includes (6)   (a) attempts to study; (b) puts in; (c) tests

30. incredible (9)   (a) ashamed; (b) unbelievable; (c) very frightening

31. jealous (10)   (a) wishing for something someone else has; (b) holding tight; (c) slim

32. melody (6)   (a) heaven; (b) tune; (c) money paid for services or privileges

33. miracle (9)   (a) a wonder; (b) cheering; (c) loss of self-control

34. novices (10)   (a) pieces broken off; (b) periods of 100 years; (c) beginners

35. ovation (8)   (a) cheering; (b) certificate given by a school at graduation; (c) position

36. panic (9)   (a) approval shown by handclapping, cheering, etc.; (b) loss of self-control brought on by fear; (c) prize

37. paradise (6)   (a) a small parade; (b) gambling equipment; (c) heaven

38. rapidly (9)   (a) hardly; (b) regularly; (c) swiftly

39. remote (6)   (a) nearby; (b) far-off; (c) unusual

40. retired (10)   (a) ashamed; (b) no longer working; (c) firmly decided on

41. scarcely (9) (a) regularly; (b) strangely; (c) hardly
42. situations (8) (a) positions; (b) prizes; (c) money paid for services or privileges
43. slender (10) (a) round; (b) slim; (c) unbelievable
44. stalled (9) (a) fell forward; (b) stopped against one's wishes; (c) grew
45. steadily (10) (a) regularly; (b) swiftly; (c) with trouble
46. terrifying (6) (a) very rapid; (b) shameful; (c) very frightening
47. toppled (10) (a) fell over; (b) went far from; (c) got free
48. transportation (10) (a) means of going from one place to another; (b) gas pedal; (c) direction
49. trophies (8) (a) pieces broken off; (b) positions; (c) prizes
50. veteran (7) (a) a grown-up person; (b) cheering; (c) a person who has served in the armed forces

---

WORD BUILDING

I. Match the word in column B to the proper word-building part in column A.

A	B
1. *cred* (9)	(a) come
2. *fec, fac, fic* (7)	(b) put, place

3. *pos, pon* (8)   (c) across
4. *trans* (10)   (d) believe, trust
5. *ven* (6)   (e) make, do

II. Choose the correct meaning for each of the words in the first column.

1. benefactor (7)   (a) a building where things are made; (b) a person who helps another; (c) a condition that brings about a good result
2. convenient (6)   (a) believing too easily; (b) certain; (c) handy
3. convention (6)   (a) a meeting; (b) trust; (c) a small window just above a door
4. credentials (9) (a) all the teachers in a school; (b) letter or certificate showing one's right to a certain position; (c) buildings where things are made
5. credibility (9) (a) believing too easily; (b) a thing that has actually happened; (c) trustworthiness
6. credit (9)   (a) a happening; (b) trust; (c) money
7. credulous (9)   (a) believing too easily; (b) completely different; (c) certain
8. discredit (9)   (a) show again; (b) keep from happening; (c) bring doubt on

9. event (6)

(a) change from one place to another; (b) a happening; (c) a meeting

10. expose (8)

(a) be against; (b) change from one language to another; (c) show

11. fact (7)

(a) trust; (b) a thing that has actually happened; (c) a condition that brings about a result

12. factor (7)

(a) a condition that brings about a result; (b) a thing that has actually happened; (c) a happening

13. factory (7)

(a) a building where things are made; (b) a place where people meet; (c) farm

14. faculty (7)

(a) a small window just above a door; (b) a person who helps another; (c) all the teachers in a school

15. invent (6)

(a) keep from happening; (b) send out; (c) produce something new

16. opposite (8)

(a) believing too easily; (b) easy to use or get to; (c) completely different

17. positive (8)

(a) different; (b) able to be seen through; (c) sure

18. prevent (6)

(a) keep from happening; (b) send out; (c) happen

19. repose (8)

(a) rest; (b) imagine; (c) bring doubt on

88

20. suppose (8)   (a) think to be true; (b) make known; (c) make new

21. transfer (10)   (a) place back; (b) change from one place to another; (c) show

22. translate (10)   (a) change relatives; (b) send out; (c) change from one language to another

23. transmit (10)   (a) produce something new; (b) think to be true; (c) send out

24. transom (10)   (a) a small window just above a door; (b) money paid to a criminal; (c) restful sleep

25. transparent (10)   (a) able to be seen through; (b) handy; (c) completely different

A Little Harder: Match the meaning in column B to the proper word in column A.

A	B
1. beneficial (7)	(a) finally
2. component (8)	(b) one to whom a debt is owed
3. creditor (9)	
4. eventually (6)	(c) leading to good
5. facsimile (7)	(d) come between
6. intervene (6)	(e) delay
7. postpone (8)	(f) enough
8. sufficient (7)	(g) change the form of
9. transform (10)	(h) temporary
10. transitory (10)	(i) a part
	(j) an exact copy

11. WOMAN MAYOR

SHOULD WOMEN ENTER POLITICS? WOULD YOU VOTE FOR A WOMAN TO BE PRESIDENT OF OUR COUNTRY?

READ ABOUT THIS WOMAN MAYOR OF A NEW JERSEY CITY.

NEW BRUNSWICK, N.J., May 31 (UPI)—When Patricia Sheehan, 33 years old, widowed mother of 3 children, became mayor of this *historic* city with a *population* of 40,000, she found out a number of interesting things:

Being a mayor, a mother and holding still another job calls for more time than there is in a 24-hour day.

Among her other duties as mayor, she must be *available* to *perform* weddings.

Her friends are *confused* about what to call her. "Hello, Pat . . . er, I mean, Mrs. Mayor . . . er, I mean, Your Honor."

City Hall was so unprepared for a woman, it took her several days to get a key to the ladies' room.

"I understand," said Mrs. Sheehan, "that I am one of the few women mayors and that I may be the youngest. I do know that I've had letters of *congratulations* from all over the country.

"I still haven't figured out how I'm going to *juggle* all my jobs, but I've always been a busy person," she said. "That'll help. The mayor's job was made to be part-time, you know."

Mrs. Sheehan will be responsible for a budget of $9,000,000 a year. Her own salary is $5,500 a year.

At home, her phone keeps ringing, her children come home from school full of stories of the day's happenings, a neighbor stops in to say, "Pat . . . er, Your Honor, I can't drive our children to school Friday. Do you think you could?" And Mrs. Sheehan makes a note in her date book to add that motherly *chore* to her many other duties.

When Mrs. Sheehan's husband died 4 years ago, she was left to attend to their 3 children, a girl, now age 9, and two boys, ages 8 and 6. She went to work for a drug company and plans to continue working for them since they will allow her to "juggle" her hours.

Mrs. Sheehan said that she had been unwilling to run for office on a ticket with five other people. "I was afraid a woman would weaken the ticket." She was *persuaded* otherwise, although she kept expecting to hear, "Why doesn't she stay home with the kids?" But not once did anyone bring that up.

"I don't think there's any *prejudice* against women in politics," Mrs. Sheehan said. "It's more a matter of men being confused. They wonder what to do with us."

—ST. LOUIS POST-DISPATCH

CHECK YOUR UNDERSTANDING

1. Another title that would best explain the main idea of this story is:
   (a) Busy Lady in City Hall
   (b) A Widow with Problems
   (c) What to Call the Mayor
   (d) Driving the Children to School
2. Mrs. Sheehan's jobs do not include
   (a) mother of 3 children.
   (b) entertainer.
   (c) mayor of the city of New Brunswick.
   (d) working for a drug company.
3. As a woman mayor, Mrs. Sheehan is
   (a) one of many women mayors in the country.
   (b) the only woman mayor in the country.
   (c) not liked by the men of the city.
   (d) possibly the youngest woman mayor in the country.
4. Mrs. Sheehan might best be described as
   (a) very busy.

(b) unfriendly.

(c) not well-liked.

(d) afraid.

5. Mrs. Sheehan says that women in politics

(a) confuse men.

(b) are better than men.

(c) are looked down on by men.

(d) make better mothers.

PUTTING THE PIECES TOGETHER

The twelve paragraphs of this story can be broken down into six main topics, or parts. Below is a title for each of these six parts. Put these titles in the same order as the parts appear in the story.

1. Mrs. Sheehan's Experience Running for Office

2. Problems of Being a Woman Mayor

3. The Mayor at Home

4. Money and the Mayor

5. Mrs. Sheehan and Other Women Mayors

6. After Her Husband's Death

WHAT'S THE REASON?

Good readers are good detectives. They see *why* things happen. See if you can find the correct *why* to complete each of these statements.

1. Mrs. Sheehan is very busy because

(a) she has three jobs.

(b) she works for a drug company.

(c) New Brunswick is an historic city.

(d) she has to perform weddings.

2. Mrs. Sheehan got letters of congratulations from all over the country because

(a) she has three jobs.

(b) she was elected mayor, even though she was a woman.

(c) she has many relatives.

(d) she will be responsible for a budget of $9,000,000 a year.

3. Mrs. Sheehan went to work for a drug company because

(a) she wanted to run for mayor.

(b) they wanted a woman to work for them.

(c) she didn't have enough to keep her busy at home.

(d) her husband died and she had to support her children.

4. Mrs. Sheehan did not wish to run for the office of mayor because

(a) she was afraid a woman would weaken the ticket.

(b) her children didn't want her to.

(c) she doesn't feel that women belong in politics.

(d) her husband had died.

IMPROVING YOUR VOCABULARY

In the first column below are the ten words in italics from the story. Pick out the best "story" meaning for each of these words.

1. *historic* city — (a) small and unimportant; (b) center of a county; (c) important in history

2. *population* of 40,000 — (a) number of houses; (b) number of years old; (c) number of people

3. *available* for duty — (a) ready for use or service; (b) can be trained; (c) able to learn

4. *perform* a wedding — (a) look for; (b) carry out, do; (c) bring people together

5. friends are *confused* — (a) mixed up; (b) excited; (c) angry and unhappy

6. letters of *congratulations* — (a) wishing a person joy; (b) advice; (c) request for help

7. *juggle* her jobs — (a) give up all at once; (b) have an exciting time; (c) keep several things going at the same time

8. another *chore* — (a) joy; (b) job; (c) reason

9. *persuaded* otherwise — (a) about to be believed; (b) unable to be convinced; (c) won over to do or believe

10. *prejudice* against women — (a) people who are against certain things; (b) an opinion formed without taking time and care to judge fairly; (c) a belief that things will finally get better

WORD BUILDING

The word *attend* is used in the above story. It means *take care of.*

Attend is built up from two word parts: *at* is a form of the prefix *ad,* meaning *towards,* while *tend* is a stem which means *stretch,* or *try.* To *attend* is to *stretch towards.* Can you see how the word has come to mean *care for?*

Usually, when you see *tend, tent* or *tens* in a word, it has the meaning of *stretch* or *try.*

Example: A *tent* is a shelter, usually of canvas, *stretched* over poles.

To Do: Match the word in column B to the proper *tend* word in column A.

A	**B**
1. *extend* his hand	(a) take care of
2. *intend* to do her work	(b) make believe; claim falsely
3. *pretend* to be ill	(c) person in charge
4. *superintendent* of the building	(d) stretch out
5. *tend* the fire	(e) plan; mean to

A Little Harder: Match the word in column B to the proper *tend* or *tens* word in column A.

A	**B**
1. *contend* for the honor	(a) thorough
2. *tense* person	(b) tough tissue connecting muscle to bone
3. *tendency* to laugh easily	(c) fight; argue; compete
	(d) a leaning in a certain

96

4. pulled a leg *tendon*   direction or way

5. *intensive* care after   (e) nervous, strained
an illness

EXPRESSING YOURSELF

1. Tell how you would feel if you were one of Mrs. Sheehan's children.

2. You are the mayor of a city with a budget of $9,000,000. Tell how you would spend the money.

3. If Mrs. Sheehan were running against a man who seemed just as good and as qualified as she was, whom would you vote for? Why?

4. Suppose you were the man who lost to Mrs. Sheehan in the election. Write a letter to her, congratulating her on her victory. You may be humorous, if you wish.

12. NEW WAYS TO FIGHT CRIME

THE CRIME RATE IN OUR COUNTRY SEEMS TO INCREASE EACH YEAR. WHAT CAN BE DONE TO REDUCE CRIME?

DO YOU THINK SOME OF THE THINGS DESCRIBED BELOW COULD BE HELPFUL?

Are we fighting crime in the Space Age with weapons from the last century?

A number of Space-Age weapons are available but are not in general use by police. For example:

• A policeman in plain clothes stands outside an apartment and holds an electronic *device* which can sniff the *odor* of illegal drugs being used inside. It can "smell" dynamite and someday may even be able to *detect* human odors.

• In a police station, a closed-circuit TV camera is trained on a row of buildings. It spots a burglar, sounds an alarm and at the same time *photographs* a white outline of the thief.

• A policeman shoots a dart from a gun into a *fleeing* purse-snatcher, who disappears into the crowd. A week later a *suspect* is brought to the police station. He is bathed with ultraviolet light. A *chemical* that had been inside the dart is used to identify him.

• A burglar sneaks up to a dark house, but fails to notice a thin wire device near the front door. Radio beams spot the man and instantly set off an alarm at the police station.

• A police officer, chasing a thief on a moonless night, loses sight of him. The policeman looks through a *special lens* and spots the suspect in the dark 500 yards away.

These are only some of the weapons available to fight crime. Why aren't they in more common use? One answer is that they are costly. Another is that devices that can detect criminals in the act may be too all-seeing and all-hearing to suit most people. Closed-circuit television may be able to watch a neighborhood more closely than most people would like. Computers—machines that store facts—may give police *information* about a person's life that ought to be nobody's business but his own.

For example, it could become impossible for a person to break the law while using an automobile and get away with it. Every car could have a special device. If a car went faster than the speed limit, that fact could be marked down by a computer and a ticket for speeding could be sent quickly through the mail.

But how many people would want such a complete car-watching, and people-watching, system?

—ALBANY TIMES-UNION

CHECK YOUR UNDERSTANDING

1. Another title that would best explain the main idea of this story is:
   (a) Using Science to Stop Crime
   (b) The Space Age
   (c) Closed-Circuit Television
   (d) A Surprised Burglar
2. This story says that one reason the weapons described are not more commonly used is that
   (a) they are unsafe.
   (b) they watch people more closely than most people would like.
   (c) they are not yet ready to be used.
   (d) they would not really work.
3. The dart described in Paragraph 5
   (a) has a chemical inside it.
   (b) will kill instantly.
   (c) disappears.

(d) bathes the person who is struck by it with
ultraviolet light.
4. The lens described in Paragraph 7
(a) helps a policeman see in the dark.
(b) can fire a bullet 500 yards.
(c) works with radio beams.
(d) can chase a thief and capture him.
5. Closed-circuit television
(a) can be used to watch a neighborhood.
(b) shows better programs than regular television.
(c) costs less than a regular television set.
(d) would be wanted by all people.

REACHING OUT

1. A weapon used to fight crime which is *not* told
about in this story is
(a) a special lens that sees in the dark.
(b) an electronic device that sniffs out certain
odors.
(c) a dart that leaves a chemical that shows
up under ultraviolet light.
(d) a chemical that puts people to sleep for a
while.
2. The wire device described in Paragraph 6 does
not
(a) open the front door automatically.
(b) work through radio beams.
(c) set off an alarm at the police station when
someone passes by it.
(d) spot anyone trying to open the front door
of the house.

USING WHAT YOU READ

Here are five devices described in the story:
(a) an electronic device that sniffs out odors
(b) closed-circuit television
(c) a dart with a chemical that shows up under ultraviolet light
(d) a wire device that spots people trying to sneak up in the dark
(e) a special lens that helps to see in the dark

Which one of these five devices would *you* use if you were in each of the following situations? Each of the five devices should be chosen only once. The first answer is done for you.

1. You are trying to find someone on a dark night. Answer: (e) The special lens that sees in the dark would be the most help here.
2. You are a policeman and think that someone inside a building is using illegal drugs.
3. You are going away from home for a week and want to make sure no burglar tries to rob your house.
4. You are a policeman in a crowd trying to capture a thief who is running away from you.
5. You live in a neighborhood where there have been many burglaries.

IMPROVING YOUR VOCABULARY

In the first column below are the ten words in italics from the story. Pick out the best "story" meaning for each of these words.

1. holds a *device* — (a) mechanical invention used for a special purpose; (b) special radio used by police; (c) a robot with keen senses

2. sniff out the *odor* — (a) sight; (b) smell; (c) sound

3. *detect* the criminal — (a) find out; (b) protect against; (c) sweeten

4. *photographs* the thief — (a) catches sight of; (b) chases after; (c) takes a picture of

5. *fleeing* purse-snatcher — (a) criminal; (b) hard to find; (c) running away from

6. *suspect* is brought in — (a) person thought to be guilty of doing wrong; (b) a criminal captured after a long chase; (c) a person in need of a bath

7. *chemical* in the dart — (a) a substance; (b) ultraviolet light; (c) a poison particularly deadly under ultraviolet light

8. *special* machine — (a) used only for seeing; (b) for a particular purpose; (c) night

9. looks into a *lens* — (a) machine; (b) piece of glass used to make things look larger and nearer; (c) a long tube used for night fighting

10. *information* about your life — (a) criminal charges; (b) temporary control; (c) facts

WORD BUILDING

The word *information* is used in the story above. It means *news,* or *knowledge.*

Information is built up from two important word parts: *in* is a prefix which means *into,* and *form* is a stem which means *shape. Information* is facts given *shape.* Can you see how the word has come to mean *news* or *knowledge?*

Usually, when you see *form* in a word, it means *form,* or *shape.*

Example: *Uniform* means having the same *form* or quality all over.

To Do: Match the word in column B to the proper *form* word in column A.

A	**B**
1. *inform* the public	(a) a rule for doing some-thing
2. *reform* a criminal	
3. *formula* for success	(b) give knowledge of something to
4. *informal* gathering	
5. *formation* of a group	(c) relaxed; not according to fixed rules
	(d) shaping; making up
	(e) improve; make better

A Little Harder: Match, as above.

A	**B**
1. *deformed* body	(a) without form
2. *conform* to society's ways	(b) misshapen
	(c) form beforehand
3. *perform* a play	(d) act according to cus-tom or rule
4. *preform* the shape	
5. *formless* mass	(e) do; act out

EXPRESSING YOURSELF

1. A congressman once said, "I think that the police should be able to listen in on every telephone call. Only the guilty people will have to worry about having their lines tapped." Tell why you agree or disagree with this congressman.

2. You receive a traffic ticket by mail saying that a computer has caught you driving over the speed limit. Tell about your feelings as you read the letter.

3. Be inventive! What kind of crime-fighting device would you like to see? In a paragraph, describe the way it would work.

4. Make up a story about a thief who thought he had committed a perfect crime but was caught because of a Space-Age weapon which the police used. Make your story one or two paragraphs long.

13. THE MARINE WHO WOULDN'T KILL

YOU ARE FIGHTING IN A WAR WITH A FELLOW SOLDIER WHO REFUSES TO SHOOT TO KILL THE ENEMY. WHAT WOULD YOU THINK OF HIM?

WHAT DO YOU THINK OF PRIVATE JONATHAN SPICER'S CONDUCT DURING THE VIETNAM WAR?

KHE SANH (AP)—Jonathan Spicer became a Marine, yet he hated war and *refused* to kill. He received the *jeers* of fellow Marines and then became a hero. He was considered dead, yet he lives today.

He was dead, field doctors said, but when he was hit while helping wounded Marines, he was just 100 yards from the main aid station. There doctors saved his life with open-heart *surgery* in a badly lighted, underground shelter.

Private Spicer, 19, of Miami, Florida, son of a former minister, once was an *outcast* at this Marine base in South Vietnam. Because of his feelings about war and killing, he was put into the medical corps. In that job he became a hero. He *repeatedly*

protected fallen men with his own body during enemy attacks.

His father said in Miami that Jonathan was "a gentle boy who even now reads his Bible every day." He said that the boy joined the Marines "only because he thought he could get into the canine division, where he could work with animals. But it didn't work out that way . . . Jonathan's great love was horses and dogs."

"What no one *realized* was that he was completely *unselfish* and wouldn't *hesitate* to put himself in danger," said a medical officer. Spicer got hit in a situation he did not have to be in. Men were having trouble loading the wounded into a *helicopter* because of enemy shelling. Spicer saw what was happening, but an officer called to him from a bunker to take cover. Nevertheless, the private ran to the helicopter. He arrived just as a shell burst near the helicopter, hitting him in the chest, face and legs.

In the medical bunker, Lieutenant John Magilligan of Brooklyn, New York, began to work on Spicer. "He died real fast," said Magilligan. "His heart stopped. So did his breathing." Nevertheless with the help of two other doctors he cut open Spicer's chest. Soon Spicer's heart began to beat again. "The heartbeat was strong, breathing was normal, blood pressure was 92. It was *remarkable,* that's all, remarkable," Magilligan said.

Spicer's youth and good physical condition worked in his favor. In all, 15 minutes had passed from the shellburst to the final stitch. Then Spicer was carried away by a Marine helicopter. A medical corpsman went along, ready to work on the heart if it stopped. It did not.

"Luck was with us," the doctor said. "I could see the hole right away. If it had been on top or in back of the heart, there would have been little chance."

—NEWSDAY

CHECK YOUR UNDERSTANDING

1. Another title that would best explain the main idea of this story is:
   (a) The Use of Helicopters in Vietnam
   (b) Life in the Marine Medical Corps
   (c) The Results of Disobeying an Officer
   (d) A Second Life for a Marine Hero
2. At first, Jonathan Spicer's fellow Marines
   (a) thought he was very brave.
   (b) were friendly to him.
   (c) looked upon him as a leader.
   (d) had nothing to do with him.
3. The chief reason we would consider Jonathan Spicer an unusual person is that
   (a) he was considered dead, yet lives today.
   (b) his father was a minister.
   (c) he was a Marine.
   (d) he loves horses and dogs.
4. Jonathan Spicer's life was saved by
   (a) open-heart surgery.
   (b) a helicopter.
   (c) his Bible.
   (d) an enemy soldier.

5. Jonathan Spicer could best be described as
   (a) cowardly.
   (b) selfish.
   (c) unselfish.
   (d) weak.

REACHING OUT

1. The one fact below that had nothing to do with Jonathan Spicer's life being saved is:
   (a) when he was wounded he was just 100 yards from the main aid station.
   (b) he was young and in good physical condition.
   (c) doctors performed open-heart surgery.
   (d) he hated war.
2. After the open-heart surgery on Jonathan Spicer, the one fact that did *not* show he was alive again was that
   (a) his chest was cut open.
   (b) his breathing was normal.
   (c) his blood pressure was 92.
   (d) his heartbeat was strong.

FIRST THINGS FIRST

Arrange these events in the order in which they happened to Jonathan Spicer.
1. He got hit by an enemy shell.
2. He was brought back to life.
3. He joined the Marines.
4. His heart and breathing stopped.

110

5. He was made fun of and not liked by his fellow Marines.

6. Doctors cut open his chest.

WHAT'S THE REASON?

Good readers are good detectives. They see *why* things happen. See if you can find the right *why* to complete each of these statements.

1. Jonathan Spicer was considered dead because
   (a) he had been hit by a shell.
   (b) his heart and breathing had stopped.
   (c) he could not move.
   (d) he had been struck in the face by parts of a shell.

2. Jonathan Spicer can be considered lucky because
   (a) the doctors could see the hole in his heart right away.
   (b) he was not put into the canine division.
   (c) he wouldn't hesitate to put himself in danger in order to save another man's life.
   (d) he was taken away on a helicopter after he had been wounded.

3. Jonathan Spicer became a hero to his fellow Marines because
   (a) he was in the medical corps.
   (b) he was operated on by a team of three doctors.
   (c) he repeatedly protected fallen men with his own body during enemy fire.
   (d) he was the son of a former minister.

4. Jonathan Spicer joined the Marines because
   (a) he hated the enemy in Vietnam.

(b) he thought he could get into the canine division.

(c) his father told him to.

(d) he wanted to be in the medical corps.

IMPROVING YOUR VOCABULARY

In the first column below are the ten words in italics from the story. Pick out the best "story" meaning for each of these words.

1. *refused* to kill — (a) made up one's mind; (b) tried very hard; (c) said "no" to

2. received *jeers* — (a) insulting remarks; (b) cheers; (c) help

3. open-heart *surgery* — (a) careful discussion of a problem; (b) temporary care of a patient; (c) treatment of an injury or disease through an operation

4. an *outcast* — (a) marine of high rank; (b) person without friends; (c) trainee

5. *repeatedly* acted — (a) once in a while; (b) often; (c) rarely

6. *realized* his bravery — (a) understood clearly; (b) hoped for; (c) spoke about

7. completely *unselfish* — (a) cowardly; (b) caring for others; (c) able to do very fine work

8. wouldn't *hesitate* (a) want to; (b) attempt; (c) stop for an instant
9. loaded into a *helicopter* (a) an aircraft lifted and moved by large horizontal propellers; (b) a large, four-engine airplane; (c) an aircraft carrier used to transport wounded soldiers
10. *remarkable* event (a) unimportant; (b) unusual; (c) unnecessary

---

WORD BUILDING

The word *pressure* is used in the story above. It means *a pushing action.*

Pressure comes from the stem *press* which means *to use force or weight against.* Usually, when you see *press* in a word, it has the meaning of *using force or weight against.*

Example: To *suppress* means to put down by *force.*

To Do: Match the word in column B to the proper *press* word in column A.

A	**B**
1. *express* your feelings	(a) make known
2. *pressing* need	(b) have a strong effect on feelings and mind
3. *depressed* by illness	(c) requiring immediate action or attention
4. an *impressive* show	(d) saddened; lowered in spirit
5. *impress* the girl	(e) holding the attention

A Little Harder: Match, as above.

	A		**B**
1.	*repress* your anger	(a)	effect produced on a person
2.	*oppress* a minority		
3.	*impressionable* young person	(b)	squeeze together
4.	*compress* your long report	(c)	keep down unjustly by cruelty
5.	make a good *impression*	(d)	easily influenced
		(e)	prevent a natural or normal activity

EXPRESSING YOURSELF

1. Who is the greater hero: a soldier who kills ten of the enemy, or a medical corpsman who protects fallen men with his own body? Why?
2. Tell about someone you know or read about who was close to death but was saved by medical science.
3. Jonathan Spicer's good physical condition helped save him. List five things a person might do to stay in good physical condition.
4. Tell about someone whom you had a low opinion of, at first, but then learned to think better of.
5. "Luck was with us," said the doctor in the last paragraph. Write a paragraph or two telling about a time luck was with you, or against you.

14. THE THINKING MACHINE

ARE ROBOTS THAT WILL DO MAN'S WORK ON THEIR WAY? SEVERAL IMAGINATIVE TV PROGRAMS HAVE SHOWN ROBOTS THINKING AS WELL AS, OR EVEN BETTER THAN, MEN. WILL THIS EVER REALLY BE SO?

READING ABOUT THIS "THINKING" MACHINE MAY HELP YOU MAKE UP YOUR MIND.

The Beast at Johns Hopkins University "thinks" for itself.

It "eats" when it gets hungry, "plays" when it feels good, "sleeps" when it's tired and "panics" when it gets into trouble.

It *roams* the halls of the laboratory and *wanders* into offices, surprising secretaries and engineers as it knocks on the door. When the Beast is hungry, it seeks out electrical wall *outlets,* plugs in, and *recharges* its 12 battery cells.

The Beast was built to survive without human help. This is exactly what it does. It looks like a very large hatbox. It has a head which can be drawn in and out and which bangs against the wall in search of outlets.

When its tiny sensors, which move along the wall's surface, "feel" the outlet, the machine plugs itself into the outlet. The Beast feeds until the batteries are fully recharged and then wanders off in a playful *mood* until it is time for dinner once more.

The Beast can avoid *obstacles,* such as wires, people and stairways. When the Beast approaches a stairway, it *shudders* and backs away. This happens because of eight little white "shoes" around its edges. The shoes *indicate* holes in the floor or a loss of balance.

As the machine nears the edge of a step, one little shoe that usually rests on the floor drops down, causing the "brain" to react and the machine to draw back.

When the machine gets tangled up in a railing with its head caught between two poles, it wiggles its head back and forth like a child's hand caught in a fence railing. Then it completely stops and goes into a "panic" before trying another way to get free. To an *observer,* the machine looks completely human as it bangs along its merry way, stopping to think or decide on the next move.

The Beast is actually the second such machine to be built. The first is a shy little machine called Ferdinand that weighs about 35 pounds. When the two are put together they look like a large collie and a small cocker spaniel rolling down the halls, sniffing at the walls for plugs and *occasionally* banging into each other.

These machines open the way for electronic devices that could explore the ocean floor, caves and other planets. The Beast has shown that machines can be made to do many of the things that man does.

—SCIENCE NEWS

CHECK YOUR UNDERSTANDING

1. Another title that would best explain the main idea of this story is:
   (a) A Machine That Walks and Eats
   (b) Exploring the Ocean Floor
   (c) Ferdinand
   (d) Johns Hopkins University
2. When the Beast gets into trouble, it
   (a) "panics."
   (b) "sleeps."
   (c) "eats."
   (d) "plays."
3. The head of the Beast
   (a) can be drawn in and out.
   (b) looks like a very large hatbox.

(c) is exactly like the head of a human being.

(d) contains electrical wall outlets.

4. In this story, Ferdinand

(a) is another name for the Beast.

(b) is compared to a large collie.

(c) is the name of a machine built after the Beast.

(d) is compared to a small cocker spaniel.

5. The Beast is important because

(a) it is now used to explore other planets.

(b) it has shown that machines can be made to do many of the things that man does.

(c) it surprises secretaries and engineers.

(d) it sometimes looks completely human.

REACHING OUT

1. The Beast does *not*

(a) feed itself at electrical wall outlets.

(b) avoid obstacles.

(c) do some of the work of a secretary.

(d) wander into offices.

2. When the Beast "eats," it does *not*

(a) fully recharge its batteries.

(b) plug itself into an outlet

(c) first feel for the outlet by means of tiny sensors.

(d) feed on the same food man does.

WHAT'S THE REASON?

Good readers are good detectives. They see *why* things happen. See if you can find the correct *why* to complete each of these statements.

1. The Beast plugs into a wall outlet to
   (a) sleep.
   (b) recharge its batteries.
   (c) play.
   (d) keep its balance.
2. The Beast was built to
   (a) survive without human help.
   (b) entertain workers at Johns Hopkins University.
   (c) give Ferdinand a friend.
   (d) show that machines cannot do what man can do.
3. The Beast bangs its head against the wall because
   (a) it "panics."
   (b) it is looking for an electrical outlet.
   (c) it is playing.
   (d) cannot avoid obstacles.
4. The Beast does not fall down stairways because
   (a) it is built to detect a loss of balance.
   (b) it is not allowed to go near them.
   (c) Ferdinand makes sure he doesn't.
   (d) it can wiggle its head back and forth.

IMPROVING YOUR VOCABULARY

In the first column below are the ten words in italics from the story. Pick out the best "story" meaning for each of these words.

1. *roams* the halls   (a) runs for a while, then walks; (b) goes about without special plan or

2. *wanders* into offices — aim; (c) takes complete charge of a situation
(a) strays; (b) wonders; (c) is taken by force

3. seeks wall *outlets* — (a) hidden places; (b) places where wall and floor meet; (c) places to put in electrical plugs

4. *recharges* its battery cells — (a) fills again with electricity; (b) makes one pay again; (c) loses energy from

5. playful *mood* — (a) friendship; (b) game played by machines; (c) state of mind or feeling

6. avoid *obstacles* — (a) people who are unfriendly; (b) something built; (c) things in the way

7. *shudders* and backs away — (a) runs away; (b) shakes; (c) falls down suddenly

8. shoes *indicate* holes — (a) point out; (b) are made of; (c) keep from

9. an *observer* of the play — (a) scientist; (b) watcher; (c) playful person

10. *occasionally* happens — (a) noisily; (b) almost always; (c) once in a while

---

WORD BUILDING

The word *indicate* is used in the story above. It means *point out,* or *direct attention to.*

Indicate is built up from two important word parts: the prefix *in,* meaning *into,* and the stem *dic,* meaning *say,* or *speak. Indicate* therefore means *speak into.* When you are speaking into somebody's ear, you are directing your words to him. Now when we use *indicate,* it means to *direct attention,* whether by words or gesture.

Usually, when you see *dic* in a word, it has the meaning of *say,* or *speak.*

Example: A *verdict* is a decision of a judge or jury.

To Do: Match the word in column B to the proper *dic* word in column A.

A	B
1. *dictate* a letter	(a) person with complete control of a country
2. *contradict* the teacher	(b) book that explains words
3. use your *dictionary*	(c) to tell for someone to write down
4. ruled by a *dictator*	(d) tell beforehand
5. *predict* tomorrow's weather	(e) say a statement is not true

A Little Harder: Match, as above.

A	B
1. *indict* for trial	(a) choice of words
2. excellent *diction*	(b) blessing
3. *abdicate* his throne	(c) law
4. obey the *edict*	(d) give up title to
5. say a *benediction*	(e) charge with a crime

EXPRESSING YOURSELF

1. Tell about three uses you could find for the robot described in this story.

2. You are a secretary or an engineer working in the office, when you see the Beast wander in. In a paragraph or two, describe your reaction the first time this happens to you.

3. Suppose that robots were trained to do all of our heavy labor. What possible danger do you see in such an arrangement?

4. Check through the want ads in your local newspaper and select ten jobs which you think that robots may be able to perform within the next fifteen years.

15. NEW YORK CITY FIRE FIGHTER

"A HERO IS SOMEONE WHO DOESN'T KNOW THE MEANING OF FEAR." DO YOU AGREE?

WHAT WOULD FIREMAN JOSHUA MURRAY SAY ABOUT IT?

Jan. 12—Yesterday, wet and *shivering,* Joshua Louis Murray was one of the hundreds of New York City firemen who have been fighting a large number of serious fires in the bitter cold of the past week. Fireman Murray did not plan to be a fireman when he grew up. He wanted to be a *detective*. Instead, at the age of 34, he is one of New York City's 13,000 firemen.

Fireman Murray is a fireman first grade attached to the Fire Department's million-dollar Super Pumper System. The Super Pumper is described as the world's largest, most powerful land fire engine. It is *capable* of pumping 36 tons of water a minute onto a fire.

Fireman Murray said he became a fireman five years ago because of the opportunity it offered. "I thought it was an interesting job," he said. "It offered good *advancement* opportunity and good job conditions."

The thought of fighting fires did not frighten Fireman Murray. One of his most *vivid* childhood recollections is watching a fire when he was 8 or 9 years old. He remembers flames shooting out of the second floor of a building and people jumping out of windows. He remembers bodies being carried out, but he does not remember seeing any firemen.

Today he talks with enthusiasm about firemen. "There's a spirit of *brotherhood* you don't find in other jobs," he said yesterday after he finished fighting a six-alarm fire, his third of the day. "There's a feeling that the guys have for each other, *especially* when there's a job to be done. You know, the importance of the job. It pulls you in. You give it your best. You don't find many guys wanting to get away from this job."

And he also knows the importance of his *equipment*. Every day he and his partner spend the first two hours of their shift going over their hoses, joints, pumps and motors to make sure they are in perfect condition.

"At the end of every day, from 7:30 to 8:30, we've got classes on fire-fighting *techniques*," he said. "That goes on for as long as you're in the department."

Fireman Murray was born in Georgia. His father was a farmer but moved to Brooklyn three years after his son's birth because he thought Negroes could find better jobs there.

At school, Joshua was a gold medal track star. He was offered scholarships at Indiana University and New York University, but he decided he was not ready for college and *enlisted* in the army.

Fighting fear is not new to Fireman Murray. During the Korean War he was a machine gunner and received two Bronze Stars. He says that there were many times when he was frightened on the battlefield. Now he has learned to live with fear. A fireman must.

—NEW YORK TIMES

CHECK YOUR UNDERSTANDING

1. Another title that would best explain the main idea of this story is:
   (a) He Wanted to Be a Detective
   (b) In Korea
   (c) A Boy from Georgia
   (d) One of the Brotherhood of Firemen

2. When Joshua Murray was a boy
   (a) he never saw a fire.
   (b) he wanted to be a detective.
   (c) he went to school in Georgia.
   (d) he wanted to be a fireman.

3. This story was written during the
   (a) winter.
   (b) spring.
   (c) summer.
   (d) fall.

4. New York City firemen
   (a) do not have to take care of their equipment.
   (b) attend daily classes on fire-fighting techniques.
   (c) work one hour a day.
   (d) have no opportunities for advancement.

5. Joshua Murray enlisted in the army because
   (a) he wanted to fight in the Korean War.
   (b) he felt he was not ready for college.
   (c) he wanted to be a fireman.
   (d) he would have a chance to run in track meets.

REACHING OUT

1. One reason Murray does *not* give for becoming a fireman is
   (a) interesting work.
   (b) good pay.
   (c) good working conditions.
   (d) opportunity for advancement.

126

2. The Super Pumper System is *not*
   (a) capable of pumping 36 tons of water a minute.
   (b) the largest land fire engine.
   (c) worth a million dollars.
   (d) one of many such systems throughout the United States.
3. From the fire he watched when he was 8 or 9 years old, Joshua Murray does *not* remember seeing
   (a) firemen.
   (b) people jumping from windows.
   (c) flames.
   (d) bodies being carried out.

FIRST THINGS FIRST

Arrange these events in the order in which they happened to Joshua Murray.
1. He enlisted in the army.
2. He became a fireman.
3. He was a track star in high school.
4. He wanted to be a detective.
5. He received two Bronze Stars.
6. His father moved to Brooklyn.

THE EDUCATED GUESS

An "educated guess" is a guess based on good reasons. For example, if you say it will rain because you see dark clouds covering the sky, that is an educated guess. However, if you say it will rain because last year it rained on the same day, that is an "uneducated guess" because it is not based on good reasons.

Good readers make educated guesses. They "read between the lines." See if you can make educated guesses here based on information in the story you have just read.

1. Firemen take good care of their equipment because
   (a) their lives depend on their equipment working right.
   (b) they have very little else to do.
   (c) they get extra pay when they do.
   (d) it keeps them from going out to fight fires.
2. Firemen have a spirit of brotherhood because
   (a) most firemen are related to one another.
   (b) they are forced to by their chiefs.
   (c) they depend upon one another in times of danger.
   (d) people will think better of them.
3. Joshua Murray has probably gotten over his boyhood ambition of being a detective because
   (a) there is no brotherhood among detectives.
   (b) detectives make less money than firemen.
   (c) detectives have no excitement in their work.
   (d) he likes being a fireman.
4. Joshua Murray was probably offered scholarships because
   (a) he was a fine student.
   (b) he was going to be a fireman.
   (c) he was enlisting in the army.
   (d) he was a track star.

IMPROVING YOUR VOCABULARY

In the first column below are the ten words in italics from the story. Pick out the best "story" meaning for each of these words.

1. be a *detective* — (a) fire fighter; (b) sergeant; (c) a person whose work is solving crimes

2. wet and *shivering* — (a) unhappy; (b) careful of danger; (c) shaking from cold

3. *capable* person — (a) person in charge; (b) able to do well; (c) strong-minded

4. *advancement* opportunity — (a) learning; (b) going ahead; (c) staying put

5. *vivid* recollection — (a) sharp and lively; (b) very painful; (c) weak and distant

6. spirit of *brotherhood* — (a) persons joined as brothers; (b) a secret organization; (c) fighting a common enemy

7. *especially* well done — (a) not noticeably; (b) particularly; (c) accidentally

8. care of *equipment* — (a) fellow workers; (b) uniforms; (c) supplies needed for the job

9. fire-fighting *techniques* — (a) companies; (b) ways followed in doing a job; (c) dangers one might meet

10. *enlisted* in the army	(a) joined; (b) was drafted; (c) promoted

---

WORD BUILDING

The word *offer* is used in the story above. It means *bring to, present*.

Offer is built up from two word parts: *of* is a form of the prefix *ob* meaning *to*, while *fer* is a stem which means *bring, bear,* or *carry*. You can easily see how *offer* means *bring to*.

Usually, when you see *fer* in a word, it has the meaning of *bring, bear,* or *carry*.

Example: To *ferry* means to *carry* across a river in a boat.

To Do: Match the word in column B to the proper *fer* word in column A.

A	**B**
1. *prefer* coffee to tea	(a) direct to
2. *refer* to the dictionary	(b) feel pain, injury or loss
3. *suffer* a loss of memory	(c) disagree
4. *conference* of mayors	(d) like more; choose before
5. *differ* with his teacher	(e) meeting

A Little Harder: Match, as above.

A	**B**
1. *fertile* ground	(a) meet with
2. draft *deferral*	(b) not caring

130

3. *confer* with her advisor

4. *circumference* of the circle

5. *indifferent* to the election

(c) able to produce plentifully

(d) postponement

(e) distance around

EXPRESSING YOURSELF

1. Fireman Murray told about the fine spirit of brotherhood which exists among firemen. Why is it very important for them to have that spirit? What other jobs promote a spirit of brotherhood?

2. Joshua Murray wanted to be a detective when he grew up. What did you want to be when you were a child?

3. Joshua Murray has a vivid recollection of a fire he saw when he was 8 or 9 years old. Tell about a vivid childhood memory you have.

4. Who would be a better fireman—a man who was completely fearless, or one who has learned to live with fear? In a paragraph, give reasons for your answer.

5. All of us have fears. Tell about a fear you have. What steps might you take to either conquer that fear or learn to live with it?

Continued on Page 24, Col

REVIEW OF LESSONS 11-15

IMPROVING YOUR VOCABULARY

Choose the correct meaning for each of the words in the first column. (The number in parentheses after each word tells you the number of the story in which the word first appeared.)

1. advancement (15)   (a) wishing a person joy; (b) treatment of an injury or a disease through an operation; (c) going ahead

2. available (11)   (a) unusual; (b) mixed up; (c) ready for use or service

3. brotherhood (15)   (a) number of people; (b) persons joined as brothers; (c) people whose work is solving crimes

4. capable (15)   (a) important in history; (b) able to do well; (c) for a particular purpose

5. chemical (12)   (a) a way followed in doing a job; (b) a substance; (c) mechanical invention used for a special purpose

6. chore (11)   (a) job; (b) insulting remark; (c) thing in the way

7. confused (11)   (a) mixed up; (b) shaking from cold; (c) sharp and lively

8. congratulations (11)   (a) wishing a person joy; (b) facts; (c) things in the way

9. detect (12)   (a) carry out; (b) stop for an instant; (c) find out

10. detective (15)   (a) a watcher; (b) a person whose work is solving crimes; (c) a person without friends

11. device (12)   (a) piece of glass used to make things look larger and nearer; (b) place to put an electrical plug; (c) invention used for a special purpose

12. enlisted (15)   (a) stopped for an instant; (b) understood clearly; (c) joined

13. equipment (15)   (a) things in the way; (b) supplies needed for a job; (c) ways followed in doing a job

14. especially (15)   (a) particularly; (b) often; (c) once in a while

15. fleeing (12)   (a) shaking from cold; (b) saying "no" to; (c) running away from

16. helicopter (13)   (a) a thing in the way; (b) an aircraft lifted and moved by large horizontal propellers; (c) something simple out of which all things are made

17. hesitate (13)   (a) stop for an instant; (b) go about without a special plan or aim; (c) fill again with electricity

18. historic (18)   (a) without self-control; (b) important in history; (c) for a particular person

19. indicate (14)   (a) point out; (b) carry out; (c) keep several things going at the same time

20. information (12)   (a) facts; (b) a way followed in doing a job; (c) supplies needed for a job

21. jeers (13)

(a) loud cheering; (b) fills again with electricity; (c) insulting remarks

22. juggle (11)

(a) keep several things going at the same time; (b) stray; (c) find out

23. lens (12)

(a) job; (b) piece of glass used to make things look larger and nearer; (c) places to put electrical plugs

24. mood (14)

(a) anger; (b) smell; (c) a state of mind or feeling

25. observer (14)

(a) watcher; (b) a person whose work is solving crimes; (c) a person who takes pictures

26. obstacles (14)

(a) things in the way; (b) places to put electrical plugs; (c) persons without friends

27. occasionally (14)

(a) often; (b) particularly; (c) once in a while

28. odor (12)

(a) smell; (b) way followed in doing a job; (c) something simple out of which all things are made

29. outcast (13)

(a) supplies needed for a job; (b) a place to put an electrical plug; (c) person without friends

30. outlets (14)

(a) people thought to be guilty of doing wrong; (b) aircraft lifted and moved by large horizontal

135

propellers; (c) places to put electrical plugs

31. perform (11) (a) carry out; (b) shake; (c) find out

32. persuaded (11) (a) mixed up; (b) won over to do or believe; (c) stopped for an instant

33. photographs (12) (a) fills again with electricity; (b) takes a picture of; (c) points out

34. population (11) (a) number of people; (b) wishing a person joy; (c) facts

35. prejudice (11) (a) caring for others; (b) going ahead; (c) an opinion formed without taking time and care to judge fairly

36. realized (13) (a) joined; (b) understood clearly; (c) kept several things going at once

37. recharges (14) (a) runs away from; (b) makes insulting remarks; (c) fills again with electricity

38. refused (13) (a) carried out; (b) said "no" to; (c) stopped for an instant

39. remarkable (13) (a) unusual; (b) for a particular purpose; (c) can be used

40. repeatedly (13) (a) often; (b) sharply; (c) once in a while

41. roams (14)

(a) points out; (b) goes about without a special plan or aim; (c) parts of a house

42. shivering (15)

(a) running away from; (b) going about without a special plan or purpose; (c) shaking from cold

43. shudders (14)

(a) strays; (b) finds out; (c) shakes

44. special (12)

(a) able to do well; (b) for a particular purpose; (c) caring for others

45. surgery (13)

(a) taking a picture of; (b) state of mind or feeling; (c) treatment of an injury or disease through an operation

46. suspect (12)

(a) person thought to be guilty of doing wrong; (b) thing or person in the way; (c) a person whose work is solving crimes

47. techniques (15)

(a) states of mind or feeling; (b) things in the way; (c) ways followed in doing a job

48. unselfish (13)

(a) mixed up; (b) caring for others; (c) can be used

49. vivid (15)

(a) important in history; (b) sharp and lively; (c) shaking from cold

50. wanders (14)

(a) strays; (b) keeps several things going at the same time; (c) carries out

WORD BUILDING

I. Match the word in column B to the proper word-building part in column A.

A	**B**
1. *dic* (14)	(a) stretch; try
2. *fer* (15)	(b) shape
3. *form* (12)	(c) use force or weight
4. *press* (13)	against
5. *tend* (11)	(d) say; speak
	(e) bring; bear; carry

II. Choose the right meaning for each of the words in the first column.

1. conference (15) (a) meeting; (b) a rule for doing something; (c) a book that explains words

2. contradict (14) (a) stretch out; (b) give knowledge to; (c) say a statement is not true

3. depressed (13) (a) holding the attention; (b) saddened; (c) free

4. dictate (14) (a) to plan; (b) to tell for someone to write down; (c) claim falsely

5. dictator (14) (a) a person who tells beforehand; (b) a person with complete control of a country; (c) a person who holds meetings

6. dictionary (14)

(a) book that explains words; (b) a rule for doing something; (c) a person with complete control of a country

7. differ (15)

(a) disagree; (b) mean to; (c) make believe

8. express (13)

(a) like more; (b) tell beforehand; (c) make known

9. extend (11)

(a) stretch out; (b) plan; (c) experience pain

10. formation (12)

(a) a rule for doing something; (b) a shaping; (c) an improvement

11. formula (12)

(a) person in charge; (b) a shaping; (c) a rule for doing something

12. impress (13)

(a) give knowledge of something to; (b) have a strong effect on feelings and mind; (c) experience pain, injury, or loss

13. impressive (13)

(a) not according to strict rules; (b) requiring immediate action or attention; (c) holding the attention

14. inform (12)

(a) like better; (b) to tell a lie to; (c) give knowledge of something to

15. informal (12)   (a) not according to strict rules; (b) giving knowledge to; (c) meaning to

16. intend (11)   (a) claim falsely; (b) disagree; (c) mean to

17. predict (14)   (a) make better; (b) stretch; (c) tell beforehand

18. prefer (15)   (a) direct to; (b) like more; (c) speak about

19. pressing (13)   (a) making known; (b) sharing; (c) requiring immediate action or attention

20. pretend (11)   (a) disagree; (b) make believe; (c) tell beforehand

21. refer (15)   (a) direct to; (b) like more; (c) improve

22. reform (12)   (a) take care of; (b) make better; (c) have a strong effect on feelings and mind

23. suffer (15)   (a) feel pain, injury, or loss; (b) disagree; (c) give knowledge of something to

24. superintendent (11)   (a) a cruel person; (b) a person who writes things down; (c) person in charge

25. tend (11)   (a) take care of; (b) speak softly to; (c) make believe

140

A Little Harder: Match the meaning in column B to the proper word in column A.

A	**B**
1. circumference (15)	(a) nervous; strained
2. confer (15)	(b) meet with
3. conform (12)	(c) thorough
4. diction (14)	(d) act according to custom or rule
5. fertile (15)	(e) do; act out
6. indict (14)	(f) prevent a natural or normal activity
7. intensive (11)	(g) charge with a crime
8. perform (12)	(h) choice of words
9. repress (13)	(i) able to produce plentifully
10. tense (11)	(j) distance around

16. THE GIRL IN THE MARATHON RACE

A MARATHON RACE IS RUN OVER A COURSE OF 26 MILES AND 385 YARDS. GIRLS: WOULD YOU LIKE TO COMPETE IN SUCH A RACE? BOYS: WOULD YOU LIKE TO MARRY A GIRL WHO COULD RUN IN AND FINISH SUCH A RACE?

READ ABOUT A GIRL WHO
DID RUN IN A MARATHON.

BOSTON—Roberta Gibb Bingay, an *attractive* 24-year-old college girl, performed what may have been the most *delightful* athletic *feat* of the year. She sneaked into the running of the Boston *Marathon,* ran the entire 26 miles and 385 yards, and finished in 3 hours and 25 minutes. This is equal to 140th place in a field of 400 men.

She was the first girl ever to run in the Boston Marathon. Some of the officials said it was a *hoax.* They said there was no proof she had run the entire route because she hadn't been checked in at the different clocking points. (Many a *rascal* has tried to avoid the difficulties of the marathon by running a short distance, riding most of the course in a car, and then getting back into the race on foot near the finish!)

Roberta came to Boston for the Marathon from San Diego, California, where she was living with her husband. She had run the hills of San Diego and then took a *rugged* 3½-day bus trip to Boston, arriving the evening before the race.

She knew that the rules did not allow women in long-distance races. Rather than be stopped before she started, she hid in the bushes a few hundred yards from the starting line. When half of the field of 400 passed, she joined the pack.

At the start, she wore a black hood so that no one would know she was a girl. Later, she took off the hood and ran in a pair of Bermuda shorts over a black bathing suit.

She said her co-runners, once they realized she was serious, kept *encouraging* her. She ran most of the race with Alton Chamberlin and finished a short distance behind him. Chamberlin, among others, disagreed with those who said that she hadn't run the whole way.

She said she had first developed an interest in running while attending school with her husband, who was a member of the track team. She often ran with him. It had long been in the back of her mind to run in the Marathon.

Roberta's feat started some talk about allowing women to compete in the race, but the Boston Marathon officials would not agree.

"She's not trying to be a *crusader* about this," said her father, who is a college chemistry professor. "She just likes to run. Actually, she was surprised and a little unhappy about all the attention she got."

Roberta is five-foot-five and has honey-blonde hair and blue eyes. "She is pretty, but she is also *muscular* and well-built and has guts," her father said.

—NEWSDAY (Long Island, N.Y.)

CHECK YOUR UNDERSTANDING

1. Another title that would best explain the main idea of this story is:
   (a) Unusual Feat of a Girl Runner
   (b) The Boston Marathon
   (c) Long-Distance Running
   (d) You Better Believe It
2. Roberta Gibb Bingay is
   (a) the winner of the Boston Marathon.
   (b) a college chemistry professor.
   (c) the first girl ever to run in the Boston Marathon.
   (d) a Boston schoolteacher.
3. When the race started, Roberta
   (a) was hiding in the bushes near the starting line.
   (b) did not know women were not allowed in the race.
   (c) ran from the starting line with the rest of the runners.
   (d) drove her car to the finish line.
4. Her co-runners
   (a) told her to drop out.
   (b) reported her to the judges.
   (c) encouraged her.
   (d) made fun of her.

5. After Roberta ran in the Boston Marathon
(a) Marathon officials agreed to let women compete in future races.
(b) she was a little unhappy about the attention she got.
(c) she promised she would never run in a marathon again.
(d) she ran in the San Diego Marathon.

REACHING OUT

1. In the Boston Marathon, Roberta did *not*
(a) wear a black hood.
(b) run in a pair of Bermuda shorts over a bathing suit.
(c) finish a short distance behind Alton Chamberlin.
(d) finish first.
2. Before coming to Boston, Roberta did *not*
(a) take a 3½-day bus trip from San Diego.
(b) write to the Boston Marathon officials saying she was going to enter the race.
(c) run the hills of San Diego.
(d) know that women were not allowed to run in long-distance races.

FIRST THINGS FIRST

Arrange these events in the order in which they happened:
1. Roberta came from San Diego for the Boston Marathon.
2. Some officials said that Roberta had not really run the entire race.

3. Roberta finished the race a short distance behind Alton Chamberlin.
4. Roberta developed an interest in running while attending school with her husband.
5. Roberta ran the hills of San Diego.
6. Roberta took off her hood and ran in Bermuda shorts.
7. Roberta hid in the bushes near the starting line.

WHAT'S THE REASON?

Good readers are good detectives. They see *why* things happen. See if you can find the correct *why* for each of these statements.
1. Some officials said that Roberta did not really run the entire race because
    (a) they had seen her drive to a spot near the finish line.
    (b) she hadn't been checked in at the various clocking points.
    (c) no girl could possibly run 26 miles.
    (d) the rules did not allow women to run.
2. Roberta wore a black hood to start the race because
    (a) it was a cold, windy day.
    (b) the rules required it.
    (c) it was part of her college uniform.
    (d) she didn't want it known that she was a girl.
3. Roberta ran in the Marathon because
    (a) she likes to run.
    (b) she wanted to be a crusader.
    (c) she was invited to.
    (d) her husband couldn't make it.

4. Roberta became interested in running because
  (a) her father was a track star.
  (b) she wanted to run in the Marathon.
  (c) she wanted to show that women could run as well as men.
  (d) her husband was a member of the track team.

5. Roberta ran the hills of San Diego
  (a) to practice for the Boston Marathon.
  (b) to get to her college.
  (c) to get to the bus that would take her to Boston.
  (d) because she was a member of her college track team.

IMPROVING YOUR VOCABULARY

In the first column below are the ten words in italics from the story. Pick out the best "story" meaning for each of these words.

1. an *attractive* girl — (a) busy; (b) pleasing to look at; (c) successful

2. a *delightful* movie — (a) joyful; (b) bright; (c) awful

3. *feat* of the century — (a) lots of food; (b) a party; (c) a great happening

4. running in the Boston *Marathon* — (a) a beautiful flower; (b) a delicious cake; (c) a long race

5. a clever *hoax* — (a) trick; (b) magic; (c) hint

6. the *rascal* caused difficulties   (a) a wild animal; (b) a dishonest person; (c) a broken tool

7. a *rugged* bus trip   (a) harsh; (b) carpeted; (c) dizzy

8. kept *encouraging* the runners   (a) making tired; (b) giving hope to continue; (c) talking loudly to

9. a *crusader* for a good cause   (a) a large fighting ship; (b) a baseball player; (c) a person who fights for a cause

10. *muscular* athlete   (a) older; (b) well-developed; (c) younger

---

WORD BUILDING

The word *attractive* is used in the story above. It means *pleasing,* or *pretty.*

Attractive is built up from two important word parts: *at* is a form of the prefix *ad* which means *towards,* and *tract* is a stem which means *draw,* or *drag.* *Attractive* therefore means *drawing you towards it.*

Usually, when you see *tract* in a word, it means *draw,* or *drag.*

Example: A *tractor* is a small motor car that *draws* along farm machinery.

To Do: Match the meaning in column B to the proper *tract* word in column A.

A	**B**
1. sign a *contract*	(a) draw toward itself
2. *extract* a tooth	(b) take away

3. *retract* a statement   (c) legal agreement
4. *subtract* the money   (d) take back
     owed   (e) take out
5. *attract* flies

A Little Harder: Match, as above.

A	**B**
1. wheels lose *traction* in the mud	(a) piece of land
	(b) drawn-out
2. a large farm *tract*	(c) pulling power
3. *detract* from his fine reputation	(d) take away
	(e) had his mind drawn away in another direction
4. *distracted* by the noise	
5. *protracted* argument	

EXPRESSING YOURSELF

1. Look up the word *marathon* in an encyclopedia. In your own words, write the story of how *marathon* got its present meaning.

2. Tell whether or not you think Roberta Bingay was justified in breaking the rules of the marathon race—in running, even though women are not allowed.

3. Why do you think women are not allowed to enter long-distance races? Is that an example of prejudice? What other story in this book told about prejudice against women?

4. "It's a man's world," declared a taxi driver, "and we'd be better off if women stayed home where they belong—cooking, cleaning, sewing, and taking care of the kids!" In a paragraph, tell why you agree or disagree.

17. GOOD SPORTSMANSHIP: OUT OF STYLE?

IS IT MORE IMPORTANT TO WIN, OR TO BE A GOOD SPORT WHILE PLAYING THE GAME?

HOW DO MOST TEEN-AGERS FEEL ABOUT GOOD SPORTSMANSHIP?

It seems that good sportsmanship is going out of *style*.

151

Youngsters feel that too many people are far more *concerned* with the final score of a contest than with how the players *achieve* it.

"Everybody likes a winner. That's the only thing that really counts. Only a jerk wants to be a perfect gentleman and lose," said a 16-year-old youth from Atlanta, Georgia.

That about sums up the thinking of 37% of the teen-agers interviewed. Many even feel that being tricky and dishonest is being "smart."

"What's so terrible about holding your *opponent* in football if you're not caught at it? If the *referee* sees you, you're stuck, but if he doesn't, you've gambled and won," noted a 17-year-old youngster from Easton, Pennsylvania.

"It's okay being a good sport if that's the way everyone else plays. But you're a sucker playing strictly according to Hoyle (according to the rules) if the other guys are not playing fair," *advised* Joe Bruno, 15, of Pittsburgh, Pennsylvania.

Most teen-agers, however, consider themselves good sports. Some *admit* to being unusually hard losers and others blame their tempers for a burst of anger during the heat of a contest, but only 8% of those questioned called themselves poor sports.

"I just can't help myself. Even if I'm playing table tennis, I get sore if I lose. I know that this is wrong but that's the way I am," admitted Peter Robb, 16, of Los Angeles.

Most youngsters seem to know several people their own age who are not good sports. 28% of the teen-agers actually thought that most of the members of their group were "lousy sports."

A 14-year-old boy in Dayton, Ohio, said, "Most kids are always cheating on the score or breaking the rules in every game they play. They lie and cheat in class, too."

From their remarks we see that most teen-agers completely dislike a poor sport. The fact that sometimes they may also be guilty of such *conduct* makes little difference. Three-fourths of the youngsters do not care to *associate* with people they consider poor sports.

Young people didn't think adults rated much higher when it came to sportsmanship.

"Most older people think that having money is the most important thing in the world. How you get it doesn't matter. I wouldn't call that very sporting," said Paul Johnson, 18, of Fort Wayne, Indiana.

One youth offered an interesting *definition* of a good sport.

"I'd say that a guy who takes a gal out and spends about 10 bucks on her without getting a good-night kiss and doesn't mind is a terrific sport!"

—NEW ORLEANS TIMES-PICAYUNE

CHECK YOUR UNDERSTANDING

1. Another title that would best explain the main idea of this story is:
   (a) Teen-Agers Look at Sportsmanship
   (b) Facts About Sports
   (c) Teen-Agers Report
   (d) America's Teen-Agers
2. The Atlanta boy in Paragraph 3 thinks

(a) it's more important to be a perfect gentle-man than to win.

(b) winning is important, but only if you play fair.

(c) winning is the only thing that counts.

(d) you should cheat only if your opponent is cheating.

3. The word "it" at the end of the second para-graph means

    (a) the final score.

    (b) methods.

    (c) youngsters.

    (d) contest.

4. Most young people thought that adults

    (a) are much better than teen-agers in sports-manship.

    (b) are much worse than teen-agers in sports-manship.

    (c) are a little worse than teen-agers in sports-manship.

    (d) are about the same or a little better than teen-agers in sportsmanship.

5. This story tells you that

    (a) most teens consider themselves bad sports.

    (b) many teens think that being tricky and dishonest is "smart."

    (c) most teens like poor sports.

    (d) all teens are good sports.

REACHING OUT

1. Most teens do *not*

    (a) consider themselves good sports.

    (b) like poor sports.

(c) know people their own age who are poor sports.

(d) like to win.

2. The boy from Easton in Paragraph 5 differs from the boy from Pittsburgh in Paragraph 6 in that

(a) he would never break the rules.

(b) he likes to win.

(c) he would cheat even if his opponent were playing fair.

(d) he would cheat even if the referee were looking.

GETTING THE NUMBER FACTS

In your reading, you are often faced with number facts which you must understand. A good reader often can understand and remember what he reads because he has made sense of the number facts. See if you have made sense of the number facts in this story.

1. About three out of every four teen-agers

(a) feel that being tricky and dishonest is "smart."

(b) think that adults are much better sports than teen-agers.

(c) think of themselves as poor sports.

(d) don't care to associate with people they consider poor sports.

2. About one out of every twelve teen-agers

(a) considers himself a good sport.

(b) considers himself a poor sport.

(c) is a sore loser.

(d) likes to win.

3. About one out of every three teen-agers
   (a) feels that being tricky and dishonest is being "smart."
   (b) does not care to associate with people they consider poor sports.
   (c) will not play fair if the other team does not play fair.
   (d) rates adults below teen-agers in sportsmanship.
4. About one out of every four teen-agers
   (a) considers himself a good sport.
   (b) dislikes poor sports.
   (c) thinks that most of the members of his group are poor sports.
   (d) never cheats in school.

IMPROVING YOUR VOCABULARY

In the first column below are the ten words in italics from the story. Pick out the best "story" meaning for each of these words.

1. a new *style*   (a) dress; (b) popular way of acting; (c) speedboat

2. *concerned* with the final score   (a) correcting; (b) pushing at; (c) having to do with

3. to *achieve* success   (a) reach by one's own effort; (b) hurt oneself; (c) sneeze at

4. your *opponent* in football   (a) person on the same side; (b) person who wins; (c) person on the other side

5. a fair *referee*   (a) judge of play at games; (b) policeman; (c) player

6. Joe Bruno *advised*   (a) held tightly; (b) told a lie; (c) told someone how to do something

7. to *admit* a lie   (a) put off; (b) say something is true; (c) write about

8. guilty of poor *conduct*   (a) way of acting; (b) business rule; (c) way of teaching

9. to *associate* with people   (a) keep company; (b) keep away from; (c) be polite with

10. an interesting *definition*   (a) agreement between two people; (b) explanation; (c) ending of a book

---

WORD BUILDING

The word *conduct* is used in the story above. It is used as a noun in the story and means *behavior,* or *way of acting.*

Conduct is built up from two word parts: *con* is a prefix meaning *together,* while *duc* is a stem meaning *lead. Conduct,* therefore, means *to lead together,* or *manage.* The way in which you manage yourself is your conduct.

Usually, when you see *duc* in a word, it has the meaning of *lead.*

Example: The word *produce* has several meanings, two of which are *show* and *make.* All the meanings of *produce* come from its original meaning—*lead forward.*

To Do: Match the meaning in column B to the proper *duc* word in column A.

A	B
1. *educate* children	(a) take away; subtract
2. *introduce* the two strangers	(b) teach
3. a dairy *product*	(c) bring together; make known to one another
4. *reduce* your weight	(d) something made
5. *deduct* your expenses	(e) make less

A Little Harder: Match, as above.

A	B
1. *abduct* the child	(a) conclude; reason out
2. *aqueduct* to the city	(b) helpful
3. *induct* into the army	(c) a large pipe for bringing water over a distance
4. *deduce* who the criminals were	(d) kidnap
5. *conducive* to good learning	(e) lead into

EXPRESSING YOURSELF

1. Let's test your sportsmanship. How would you behave in the following situations? Give reasons for your actions.

   (a) At an important basketball game, the star of the opponent's team loses his contact lens, and you find it. Would you return it to him?

(b) You are pitching for your school's baseball team. A friend tells you that by rubbing vaseline on the ball you can strike out many batters. Would you do it?

(c) You notice that a football referee has made a mistake, giving your team an additional chance to score. Would you call it to his attention?

2. Do you agree with the boy from Dayton, Ohio, who said that most kids "lie and cheat in class"? What is the usual reason students give for cheating on tests?

3. Prepare a three-minute speech to be delivered in your English class on one of the following topics:

I'm a Good Sport
I Hate to Lose

4. "Having money is the most important thing in the world." Do you agree? If not, what is?

5. Find out where the expression, "according to Hoyle," comes from.

6. "Everybody likes a winner. That's the only thing that really counts." Write a paragraph telling why you agree or disagree with this statement.

18. THE CHEFS' FINAL EXAM

HOW WOULD YOU LIKE TO EAT YOUR FINAL EXAM?

THESE STUDENTS DID!

Final exams for 17 students of Milwaukee Institute of Technology were held one morning this week in Room 662. Two long tables, covered with fresh, white linen and decorated with white lilac, held nine dessert items and eight *entree* courses, each carefully *labeled*.

Starting with the entrees, the mouth-watering list read: "Chateaubriand with Mushroom Sauce," "Filet de Sole Marguery," "Roast Duckling," "Sautéed Breast of Chicken on Toast Points," "Sauerbraten," "Roast Cornish Hen," "Chicken Kiev with Brown Sauce," "Chicken Paprikash and Spaetzle."

The dessert table held these *delicacies* which looked as good to eat as their names: "Napoleon Slices," "French Pastry," "Cream Puff Swans and Eclairs," "Ice Cream Cake with Strawberry Sauce," "Neapolitan Slices," "Fruit Tartlets," "Black Forest Cherry Torte," "Lemon Meringue Custard Pie."

Each of the entrees and desserts had been prepared that morning in the kitchen and bakery of the school by the 17 students in the course called Gourmet Cookery.

Each student was to be marked on his work by 3 food experts, who would nibble a slice from each dish and score it for makeup, *appearance, aroma,* flavor and *originality* of *display.*

The white-capped students, in their last week of a 2-year course in restaurant and hotel cookery, had carefully laid out their displays on the tables and returned to the kitchen to wait for the results.

On orders from their teacher, a silver-haired French *chef* named Robert Angelvin, the students had not been allowed to work with each other in the *preparation* of their dishes.

To judge from the calm, expert way in which the young chefs whipped their sauces and tossed their salads, they had learned well under Angelvin's instruction.

Just to be in the class is an honor in itself, for the Institute is one of the very few schools in the country which has a 2-year course especially set up to train chefs. This year, all the students were male, although there have been female chefs in the past.

Other schools have courses in restaurant and hotel management but not advanced training in cooking and baking. For that reason, students in Angelvin's class come from as far away as New Mexico and the east coast.

The judges moved slowly from dish to dish, slicing here, nibbling there. By the time all 3 judges had tasted each item, only a small part of the entrees and desserts had been eaten. Since the students pay for the *ingredients,* the judges were unwilling to eat too much. When the judges were finished, the students took their entrees and desserts home.

It's the only exam a student could take, and then eat, too.

—MILWAUKEE JOURNAL

CHECK YOUR UNDERSTANDING

1. Another title that would best explain the main idea of this story is:
   (a) A Final Test That's Good To Eat
   (b) The Only School of Its Kind
   (c) Names for Food
   (d) 17 Students
2. Sauerbraten is
   (a) the nickname of the teacher of the class.
   (b) a dessert.
   (c) a salad.
   (d) an entree.

3. Milwaukee Institute of Technology's 2-year course to train chefs
   (a) is the only one of its kind in the country.
   (b) is open only to men.
   (c) does not have advanced courses in cooking and baking.
   (d) has students from New Mexico and the east coast.

4. This exam was unusual because
   (a) the students did not receive a mark.
   (b) the students could eat it.
   (c) the students were nervous.
   (d) 17 students took it.

5. The second and third paragraphs would make most people want to
   (a) study.
   (b) write.
   (c) eat.
   (d) fight.

REACHING OUT

1. The judges did *not* grade the food for
   (a) flavor.
   (b) appearance.
   (c) amount of time taken to prepare it.
   (d) originality of display.

2. The judges did *not*
   (a) take home the food they did not eat.
   (b) taste each item.
   (c) eat only a small part of the entrees and desserts.
   (d) move slowly.

WHAT'S THE REASON?

Good readers are good detectives. They see *why* things happen. See if you can find the right *why* to complete each of these statements.

1. Students come to the Milwaukee Institute of Technology from as far away as New Mexico because
   - (a) it is easy to be admitted to the school.
   - (b) Milwaukee is famous for its food.
   - (c) there are no schools in New Mexico.
   - (d) it is one of the few schools with a special course to train chefs.

2. The judges ate only a small part of the food because
   - (a) they were not hungry.
   - (b) the students had paid for the ingredients.
   - (c) the food was so badly prepared.
   - (d) the judges could then take the uneaten food home.

3. Most of the students in the chef-training course are male because
   - (a) the school does not like female students.
   - (b) girls do not like to cook.
   - (c) most chef jobs go to men.
   - (d) the teacher is a man.

4. In the preparation of their dishes, the students were not allowed to work with each other because
   - (a) they were to receive grades on their own work.
   - (b) "too many cooks spoil the broth."
   - (c) Robert Angelvin does not like students cooperating with one another at any time.

(d) they had argued with one another too frequently.

IMPROVING YOUR VOCABULARY

In the first column below are the ten words in italics from the story. Pick out the best "story" meaning for each of these words.

1. eight *entree* courses — (a) training method; (b) a dish served as a main meal; (c) dessert
2. *labeled* their work — (a) planned; (b) searched; (c) marked
3. food *delicacies* — (a) blueberry pancakes; (b) supermarkets; (c) choice kinds of food
4. a neat *appearance* — (a) outward look; (b) overcoat; (c) costume
5. *aroma* of coffee — (a) sight; (b) smell; (c) sound
6. judged for *originality* — (a) ability to say words correctly; (b) ability to speak clearly; (c) ability to think up new ideas
7. *display* of products — (a) poor show; (b) contest; (c) show
8. the *chefs* tossed the salad — (a) cooks; (b) generals; (c) boy scouts
9. *preparation* of a meal — (a) cleaning up; (b) making ready; (c) eating of
10. *ingredients* of a pudding — (a) parts of a mixture; (b) small lumps; (c) number of servings

WORD BUILDING

The word *final* is used in the story above. It means *the last*. *Final* comes from the stem *fin* which means *end,* or *limit*. Usually, when you see *fin* in a word, it means *end* or *limit*.

Example: The word *finish* means to *complete,* or make an *end* of.

To Do: Match the meaning in column B to the proper *fin* word in column A.

A	B
1. *define* the word	(a) certain
2. *confine* to quarters	(b) one who is in the last part of a contest
3. *finalist* in the 60-yard dash	(c) shut up; keep within limits
4. *refine* your work	(d) make perfect
5. *definite* views on life	(e) state the meaning of

A Little Harder: Match, as above.

A	B
1. *infinite* space	(a) explanation of what something means
2. *finale* of the show	(b) uncertain; unsure
3. a clear *definition*	(c) endless; very great
4. *unrefined* sugar	(d) not pure
5. at some *indefinite* time	(e) last part of a musical work

166

EXPRESSING YOURSELF

1. Make up a menu for a meal of your favorite foods.
2. Write a short letter to the cook or the manager of your school's lunchroom. Tell her that you read this article and you want to know whether she recommends a chef's job for boys and girls, how much money you could earn, etc
3. In the "Education" section of your Sunday newspaper you will find schools which offer special training, such as the Milwaukee Institute of Technology. Draw up a list of the different schools and the careers for which they prepare their students.

19. COURAGEOUS COED

DO YOU SOMETIMES FEEL THAT YOU HAVE MORE TO COMPLAIN ABOUT THAN MOST OTHER PEOPLE?

WOULD YOU WANT TO TRADE PLACES WITH EMMA FLORES?

Never say "no" to Emma Flores. It isn't in her vocabulary.

People have been trying to say no to Emma

ever since she was *crippled* by polio at age 11. "No, you can't get out of bed . . . No, you can't walk . . . No, you can't go to school . . ."

But Emma always said, "Yes, I can." People began to believe her. A great number of believers, in fact, were present when Emma received her diploma from college.

Now 22, the pretty brunette with big brown eyes can walk but will never have the use of her arms and hands. She is thankful to her schoolmates for making it possible for her to live her day-to-day life at college. Teams of girls helped her get up in the morning and dress, carried her books, fed her each mouthful of food and even tucked her into bed at night—the bed next to a respirator * which hums and sighs all night long, doing Emma's breathing for her while she sleeps. The girls washed out Emma's things, ironed her blouses, helped her shop and gave her rides.

Emma did all the rest. She learned to write with her feet, *grasping* the pencil between two toes. That's how she took notes in class. She typed her reports, using a pencil held in each foot to strike the keys. Earning A's and B's, she majored in languages and added to the money she received from a scholarship by *tutoring* other students.

She put worry out of her life. Although she *depends* on others, she doesn't give it much thought.

"I just walk into the cafeteria," Emma said, "not knowing from one meal to the next who's going to help me. But somebody always does. I don't worry about it."

Emma treats the use of her feet like a rare

* respirator—a device to aid breathing

gift. "I really enjoy using my feet," she said. "I have a ball. I learned to paint—with watercolors —and when I want the colors to run together I have to hold up the paper and shake it with both feet. It's a riot."

Although Emma doesn't need a respirator in the daytime, she must have one at night, so she takes a *portable* machine with her when she travels. During her vacation she flew to New York alone, to visit a friend, and this summer she plans to take a trip to Mexico.

Emma is a native of Mexicali, where her parents still live. She was one of many Mexican children stricken by polio at a time when doctors there could not even *identify* it. Her father was told that Emma would be bedridden the rest of her life. He refused to accept the *verdict*.

With nothing but *determination* on his side, he tried in every way to help his daughter. After a series of operations, Emma *progressed* from getting about with a wheelchair, to braces,* to walking on her own.

While other students were getting graduation presents, Emma was giving one—an art scrapbook she had carefully and painfully put together for her friend, Sandy McIntyre, "the girl who helped me the most."

She used magazine cutouts to *illustrate* carefully lettered quotations about life and love. The bookends with these words: "Thank you for life, thank you for grace, thank you, Lord, thank you."

—LOS ANGELES TIMES

* braces—supports for a weak part of the body

170

CHECK YOUR UNDERSTANDING

1. Another title that would best explain the main idea of this story is:
   - (a) Typing with Feet
   - (b) A Handicapped Girl Succeeds
   - (c) Scrapbook from Life
   - (d) Polio and Its Effects

2. Emma Flores
   - (a) worries a great deal.
   - (b) cannot walk.
   - (c) writes with her feet.
   - (d) feeds herself.

3. Emma uses a respirator
   - (a) to help her breathe at night.
   - (b) at all times.
   - (c) to help her type.
   - (d) only during the day.

4. When Emma was a young girl in Mexicali,
   - (a) Mexican children never got polio.
   - (b) doctors knew a great deal about polio.
   - (c) she was the only child there to come down with polio.
   - (d) she was one of many Mexican children struck by polio.

5. Emma Flores is
   - (a) selfish.
   - (b) determined.
   - (c) complaining.
   - (d) worrying.

REACHING OUT

1. Emma's schoolmates in college did *not*
   (a) feed her.
   (b) wash and iron for her.
   (c) help her dress.
   (d) take notes in class for her.
2. In college, Emma did *not*
   (a) earn grades of A's and B's.
   (b) tutor other students.
   (c) find herself without friends.
   (d) major in languages.

FIRST THINGS FIRST

Arrange these events in the order in which they happened to Emma Flores.

1. She was stricken with polio.
2. She made a scrapbook as a present for Sandy McIntyre.
3. She lived in Mexicali.
4. She learned to use a wheelchair.
5. She taught herself to walk again.
6. She typed her college reports with her feet.

WHAT'S THE REASON?

Good readers are good detectives. They see *why* things happen. See if you can find the right *why* to complete each of these statements.

1. Emma is thankful to her college schoolmates because
   (a) they did all her homework for her.
   (b) they gave her a scrapbook for graduation.
   (c) they helped her walk.
   (d) she would never have gotten through college without their help.
2. Emma learned to write with her feet because
   (a) she can write faster with them than she can with her hands.
   (b) she enjoys doing unusual things.
   (c) she had already learned to use her feet to type.
   (d) she cannot use her hands at all.
3. Emma tutored other students because
   (a) language majors have to tutor.
   (b) she needed money to help get through college.
   (c) she needed to feel important.
   (d) it kept her mind off her worries.
4. Emma made a scrapbook for Sandy McIntyre because
   (a) she was grateful for the help Sandy had given her.
   (b) Sandy had made one for her.
   (c) Sandy needed it for a class she was taking.
   (d) it was a requirement for graduation.

IMPROVING YOUR VOCABULARY

In the first column below are the ten words in italics from the story. Pick out the best "story" meaning for each of these words.

1. *crippled* by illness (a) made strong; (b) made proud; (c) weakened

2. *grasping* the pencil (a) pointing; (b) sharpening; (c) taking tight hold of

3. *tutoring* other students (a) passing; (b) teaching; (c) hiring

4. *depends* on others (a) needs help from; (b) works for; (c) steals from

5. a *portable* typewriter (a) able to be moved; (b) unable to be moved; (c) a special table for

6. *identify* a child (a) recognize; (b) cure; (c) bring up

7. accept the *verdict* (a) reward; (b) truth; (c) decision

8. *determination* to get well (a) planning; (b) firm decision; (c) giving up

9. *progressed* with hard work (a) got worse; (b) got better; (c) remained the same

10. to *illustrate* a story (a) write; (b) make a song of; (c) make a picture for

---

WORD BUILDING

The word *vocabulary* is used in the story above. It means *all the words used by a person.*

Vocabulary comes from the stem *voc* meaning *call,* or *speak.* Usually when you see *voc* or *vok* in a word, it has the meaning of *call* or *speak.*

174

Example: To *vocalize* means to *speak,* or *sing.*

To Do: Match the meaning in column B to the proper *voc* or *vok* word in column A.

	A		**B**
1.	choose a *vocation*	(a)	be in favor of
2.	hear a fine *vocalist*	(b)	hobby
3.	*revoke* your license	(c)	career; trade; occu-pation
4.	*advocate* a change		
5.	keep busy with an *avocation*	(d)	take away; withdraw
		(e)	singer

A Little Harder: Match, as above.

	A		**B**
1.	*evoke* a reply	(a)	noisy
2.	*invoke* the judge's mercy	(b)	anger; irritate; ex-cite
3.	*provoke* bad feelings	(c)	hesitate
4.	*equivocate* in deciding	(d)	ask for help
5.	*vociferous* cries	(e)	call forth; bring out

EXPRESSING YOURSELF

1. The story of Emma Flores could give hope to a person with problems. Tell about someone you know who might be helped by reading about Emma. Tell why.
2. Emma's father refused to admit defeat. Tell about some father you know who has helped his child overcome a trouble or handicap.

3. Emma had polio, a disease which has been all but wiped out in America. In an encyclopedia, look up the story of polio and the Salk vaccine. Then tell the class what you found out.

4. Emma is quoted as using slang expressions such as "have a ball" and "It's a riot." What are some of the slang expressions you and your friends use? Discuss how these expressions came to have their present meanings.

5. Emma has put worry out of her life. She has faith that things will work out. In a paragraph, tell whether or not you think it is good not to worry. Give reasons.

20. BLIND FBI MAN

LIKE EMMA FLORES, THERE ARE MANY
SUCCESSFUL PEOPLE WHO HAVE
PHYSICAL HANDICAPS. HELEN KELLER
COULDN'T SEE, SPEAK, OR HEAR. HOW
CAN PEOPLE STILL DO WORTHWHILE
WORK UNDER SUCH CIRCUMSTANCES?

YOU ARE ABOUT TO LEARN HOW EMORY
GREGG OVERCAME HIS HANDICAP.

One of the most remarkable untold stories in
the files of the Federal Bureau of Investigation is

the case history of Emory Gregg, who went blind 9 years ago and now uses memory in place of eyes to track down enemy agents.

Mr. Gregg had taken part in some of the biggest spy cases during and after World War Two. His work had brought praise from J. Edgar Hoover, head of the FBI.

One morning Mr. Gregg woke up blind, with blood coming out of his eyes. Afterwards, he could no longer read, drive an automobile, or *recognize* a face at close range. *Physicians* cut pinholes in his retinas,* but this gave him only a field of vision of 7 inches at a distance of 20 feet, smaller at closer range.

Mr. Gregg spent a long and painful *convalescence,* fearing the day he would have to report back to work, where sharp vision was so important. He had been a crack pistol shot and a weapons instructor.

The day came for him to see Mr. Hoover.

"It turned out to be one of the happiest days of my life," Mr. Gregg said. "Mr. Hoover told me that he wanted me to stay on. He said that I would be judged not on any medical report but on how I performed. I walked out of that room determined to do my job better than any other man."

Details of the work Mr. Gregg has performed since that day cannot be told. It can be told, however, that he has had two *promotions* and is now a high officer in the FBI.

Since he can see only *faintly* through the pinholes cut in his retinas, Mr. Gregg depends mainly on his thinking powers. Written material is read

* retinas—back parts of the eyes on which the picture is formed.

aloud to him, photographs are described to him. His memory, very sharp to make up for his poor vision, files each fact. At his mental "fingertips" he keeps track of every known *foreign* agent in the United States.

"He is truly a walking *encyclopedia*," one of Mr. Gregg's friends said. "He can talk by the hour, presenting the most detailed information about spying."

Mr. Gregg himself says, "What seemed at first like an impossible handicap has turned out the other way. I don't have to depend on notes and files of paper! I find myself able to recall faces of criminals, names, dates, phone numbers and endless other facts as far back as my earliest days with the FBI."

Today he plays fairly good golf, using clubs painted *luminous* white. Members of his foursome tell him in which direction and how far to shoot. He cannot see where the ball goes. The others show him.

Mr. Gregg wears no glasses, carries no cane and walks without hesitation along FBI hallways. He is proud of the fact that many people who know him do not realize that he is blind. In conversation, he seems to be looking into the other person's eyes. It is *startling* to be told, "I have no idea what you look like."

—NEW YORK TIMES

CHECK YOUR UNDERSTANDING

1. Another title that would best explain the main idea of this story is:

(a) Counter-Spying
(b) The FBI
(c) A Walking Encyclopedia
(d) An Unusual Member of the FBI
2. Emory Gregg's present work for the FBI is
   (a) completely secret.
   (b) training handicapped agents.
   (c) training agents in the use of arms.
   (d) dealing in special matters of spying.
3. After his bleeding, Emory Gregg could still
   (a) see faintly.
   (b) shoot a pistol.
   (c) follow the course of a golf ball.
   (d) read.
4. Mr. Gregg has found that his handicap
   (a) is a help in his work.
   (b) is impossible to overcome.
   (c) has made him weak.
   (d) is a tiring experience.
5. A crack pistol shot can
   (a) fix pistols.
   (b) load pistols quickly.
   (c) fire pistols well.
   (d) work in dangerous places.

REACHING OUT

1. Emory Gregg does *not*
   (a) play golf.
   (b) wear glasses.
   (c) depend mainly on his thinking powers.
   (d) have a good memory.
2. Emory Gregg's first feeling about his blindness might be called

(a) hopeful.
(b) happy.
(c) angry.
(d) fearful.

FIRST THINGS FIRST

Arrange these events in the order in which they happened:
1. Mr. Gregg had bleeding in his eyes.
2. Mr. Gregg was a crack pistol shot.
3. J. Edgar Hoover encouraged Mr. Gregg when he returned to the FBI.
4. Mr. Gregg developed a very sharp memory.
5. It took a long time for Mr. Gregg to recover from his operation.

WHAT'S THE REASON?

Good readers are good detectives. They see *why* things happen. See if you can find the right *why* to complete each of these statements.
1. J. Edgar Hoover kept Mr. Gregg on the job with the FBI because
   (a) he could fire a gun well.
   (b) he passed his medical exam.
   (c) he felt sorry for him.
   (d) he performed better than other men.
2. Emory Gregg was afraid to return to his FBI job because
   (a) he would be in trouble with Mr. Hoover.
   (b) he thought he would not be able to work for the FBI anymore.

(c) he had to be trained from the beginning.

(d) he couldn't drive a car.

3. Though he lost most of his vision, Emory Gregg was successful with the FBI because

(a) he did only special jobs.

(b) he had an excellent memory.

(c) his secretary read all the material to him.

(d) Mr. Hoover liked him.

4. Mr. Gregg thought that his blindness was *not* such a serious handicap because

(a) he could still play golf.

(b) he had a good memory.

(c) he cracked a big spy case.

(d) he got help from other agents.

5. Details in the work of Mr. Gregg cannot be told because

(a) everybody already knows them.

(b) they have not yet been completed.

(c) they are secret information for FBI files.

(d) the author of the story doesn't want to tell them.

IMPROVING YOUR VOCABULARY

In the first column below are the ten words in italics from the story. Pick out the best "story" meaning for each of these words.

1. *recognize* a face   (a) greet; (b) hate; (c) identify

2. examined by *physicians*   (a) doctors; (b) dentists; (c) athletes

3. a long *convalescence* for illness — (a) terrible shaking; (b) rest to get back one's health; (c) dangerous operation

4. *details* of the work — (a) small parts; (b) odds and ends; (c) large parts

5. *promotion* for good work — (a) getting ideas; (b) moving ahead; (c) working for

6. sees *faintly* — (a) clearly; (b) far away; (c) not clearly

7. a *foreign* agent — (a) having to do with the armed forces; (b) having to do with another country; (c) having to do with finding a job

8. *encyclopedia* of art — (a) a set of books giving information arranged in alphabetical order; (b) a collection; (c) a painting

9. painted *luminous* white — (a) dull; (b) clear; (c) shining

10. a *startling* happening — (a) noisy; (b) surprising; (c) square

---

WORD BUILDING

The word *conversation* is used in the story above. It means a *talking together.*

Conversation is built up from two main word parts: the prefix *con* meaning *together,* and the stem *vers* meaning turn. Can you see how the word *conversation* has come to mean *talking together?*

183

Usually, when you see *vers* or *vert* in a word, it has the meaning of *turn*.

Example: An *anniversary* is the yearly re*turn* of the date of some event, such as a wedding.

To Do: Match the meaning in column B with the proper *vers* or *vert* word in column A.

A	**B**
1. *reverse* direction	(a) straight up and down
2. *advertise* in the newspaper	(b) change to the opposite
3. a *vertical* line	(c) call public attention to
4. heated *controversy*	(d) opponent
5. up against a strong *adversary*	(e) argument; quarrel; debate

A Little Harder: Match, as above.

A	**B**
1. *avert* a strike	(a) unfavorable; opposed
2. *convert* to your viewpoint	(b) go back
3. an *inadvertent* error	(c) turn aside; prevent
4. *adverse* ruling by the judge	(d) change
5. *revert* to his old ways	(e) due to lack of attention or oversight

---

EXPRESSING YOURSELF

1. The devotion of Annie Sullivan, the teacher of Helen Keller, was written about in a play entitled, "The Miracle Worker." Annie succeeded in helping Helen because she believed that handicapped persons should not be treated like "a box of eggs." What did Annie mean? Tell why you agree or disagree with her.

2. The Lighthouse for the Blind is a private agency that helps blind people by teaching them special job skills and selling their products. Write a letter to the agency requesting information about the things they sell and the types of skills they teach.

3. Have one student in the class play the role of J. Edgar Hoover. Have another play the role of Emory Gregg. Have them act out their meeting as it is told in the story.

4. Tell about another blind person who overcame his handicap.

Coincidence

Continued on Page 24, Co

REVIEW OF LESSONS 16-20

IMPROVING YOUR VOCABULARY

Choose the correct meaning for each of the words in the first column. (The number in parentheses after each word tells you the number of the story in which the word first appeared.)

1. achieve (17) (a) cough; (b) hurt; (c) do, accomplish

2. admit (17) (a) confess; (b) lie; (c) scream

3. advised (17) (a) tried; (b) told how to act; (c) tricked

4. appearance (18) (a) how one is heard; (b) when one leaves; (c) how one is seen by others

186

5. aroma (18)   (a) see; (b) smell; (c) touch

6. associate (17)   (a) join with friends; (b) break up; (c) join the army

7. attractive (16)   (a) terrible to look at; (b) sticking to; (c) nice to look at

8. chefs (18)   (a) bosses; (b) cooks; (c) salads

9. concerned (17)   (a) quiet; (b) having to do with; (c) seeing for

10. conduct (17)   (a) way of behaving; (b) way of dressing; (c) way of fighting

11. convalescence (20)   (a) health rest; (b) headache; (c) fever

12. crippled (19)   (a) made well; (b) made lame; (c) straightened out

13. crusader (16)   (a) poor loser; (b) winner; (c) fighter for a cause

14. definition (17)   (a) ending; (b) education; (c) meaning

15. delicacies (18)   (a) special kinds of food; (b) frankfurters; (c) lunches

16. delightful (16)   (a) sad; (b) enjoyable; (c) bright

17. depends (19)   (a) gives help to; (b) needs help from; (c) takes time

18. display (18)   (a) layout; (b) a bad sport; (c) anger

19. details (20)   (a) little parts; (b) big parts; (c) chapters

20. determination (19)

(a) firm decision; (b) weak decision; (c) a long wait

21. encouraging (16)

(a) giving hope; (b) holding back; (c) selling short

22. encyclopedia (20)

(a) dictionary; (b) set of books with information arranged alphabetically; (c) table of contents

23. entree (18)

(a) opening; (b) main part of a meal; (c) dessert

24. faintly (20)

(a) proudly; (b) correctly; (c) unclearly

25. feat (16)

(a) an unusual act; (b) a party; (c) an award

26. foreign (20)

(a) about our country; (b) about mountains; (c) about another country

27. grasping (19)

(a) letting go; (b) holding tightly; (c) breathing badly

28. hoax (16)

(a) trick; (b) horse; (c) agreement

29. identify (19)

(a) point out; (b) pick up; (c) pay back

30. illustrate (19)

(a) take pictures; (b) draw pictures; (c) prepare

31. ingredients (18)

(a) water; (b) salad; (c) things in a mixture

32. labeled (18)

(a) sued; (b) swept; (c) marked

33. luminous (20)

(a) like a metal; (b) dark; (c) shining

34. marathon (16)   (a) a long race; (b) a war; (c) a parade

35. muscular (16)   (a) poorly developed; (b) well-developed; (c) weak

36. opponent (17)   (a) enemy; (b) friend; (c) person playing against you

37. originality (18)   (a) ability to make decisions; (b) ability to think up new ways; (c) ability to organize

38. physicians (20)   (a) doctors; (b) lawyers; (c) teachers

39. portable (19)   (a) heavy; (b) able to be carried; (c) having windows

40. preparation (18)   (a) making ready; (b) mixture; (c) getting away

41. promotions (20)   (a) advances; (b) failures; (c) holidays

42. progressed (19)   (a) moved back; (b) improved; (c) informed

43. rascal (16)   (a) a trusted helper; (b) a troublemaker; (c) a beginner

44. recognize (20)   (a) explain; (b) improve; (c) identify

45. referee (17)   (a) a game judge; (b) a gym teacher; (c) a free pass

46. rugged (16)   (a) rough; (b) smooth; (c) carpeted

47. startling (20)   (a) amazing; (b) uninteresting; (c) exciting

48. style (17)   (a) model; (b) action; (c) fashion

49. tutoring (19)   (a) learning; (b) dressing; (c) instructing

50. verdict (19)   (a) opinion; (b) law; (c) truth

WORD-BUILDING PARTS

Match the word in column B to the proper word-building part in column A.

A	**B**
1. *voc* (19)	(a) turn
2. *vers, vert* (20)	(b) call; speak
3. *fin* (18)	(c) draw; drag
4. *duc* (17)	(d) end; limit
5. *tract* (16)	(e) lead

WORD-BUILDING VOCABULARY

Choose the right meaning for each of the words in the first column.

1. advertise (20)   (a) call public attention to; (b) buy; (c) talk about

2. attract (16)   (a) give away; (b) let up; (c) draw to

3. confine (18)   (a) make sweet; (b) open; (c) lock up

4. contract (16)   (a) legal agreement; (b) payment; (c) piece of land

5. controversy (20)   (a) capturing; (b) argument; (c) thought

6. deduct (17)   (a) put back; (b) let go; (c) take away

7. define (18)   (a) pay a fine; (b) write a sentence; (c) state the meaning of

8. definite (18)   (a) uncertain; (b) certain; (c) perfect

9. educate (17)   (a) teach; (b) learn; (c) reward

10. extract (16)   (a) give to; (b) take out; (c) take back

11. introduce (17)   (a) bring together; (b) hate; (c) separate

12. product (17)   (a) vegetable; (b) something made; (c) addition

13. reduce (17)   (a) make more; (b) make less; (c) drive

14. refine (18)   (a) make perfect; (b) make a mistake; (c) copy

15. reverse (20)   (a) do the same; (b) go up; (c) change to the opposite

16. revoke (19)   (a) be in favor of; (b) do away with; (c) make noise

17. subtract (16)   (a) take out; (b) put in; (c) take to

18. vertical (20)   (a) straight across; (b) straight up and down; (c) crooked

19. vocalist (19)   (a) singer; (b) cello; (c) piano player

20. vocation (20)   (a) rest; (b) illness; (c) career

A Little Harder: Match the meaning in column B to the proper word in column A.

	A		B
1.	abduct (17)	(a)	anger
2.	avert (20)	(b)	change
3.	convert (20)	(c)	prevent
4.	deduce (17)	(d)	pulling power
5.	definition (18)	(e)	conclude
6.	finale (18)	(f)	lead to
7.	induct (17)	(g)	kidnap
8.	infinite (18)	(h)	endless
9.	provoke (19)	(i)	explanation
10.	traction (16)	(j)	end of a musical show

21. JIM McMILLAN

WHICH IS MORE IMPORTANT FOR ATHLETIC SUCCESS: NATURAL ABILITY OR LONG HOURS OF PRACTICE?

WHICH WAS MORE IMPORTANT FOR JIM McMILLAN?

"There were these kids playing cards and drinking in the park, and a bunch of us were playing basketball," Jim McMillan recalled. "I guess the game was over and the guys went over to watch the card game. They weren't going to play. We never had any money in our pockets. I stayed on the court, fooling around by myself. A car drove up, and some guys got out. One of them started shooting the ball up with me and talking to me.

"Pretty soon it turned out they were cops and took everybody but me away in the paddy wagon. Lots of times I've watched those card games. This time I was playing basketball. I was lucky."

Jim McMillan says that basketball kept him out of trouble. "Other kids liked to show how much man they were. Basketball was my *obsession*."

The Ivy League consists of the country's oldest and finest colleges. Jim McMillan of Columbia may be the most important Negro athlete the Ivy League ever had. But Jim attended the first 8 grades in a *segregated* school in North Carolina, where he was born.

Then his mother moved with Jim and his younger brother to Brooklyn. Jim was in the eighth grade and he was already six feet one inch tall, but the coach at Junior High 64 had to show him what a layup was. He had never even had a pair of sneakers on before.

"All summer after that I'd be in the playgrounds playing ball. I was too young to get a job, even though we needed the money. I'd play all day, go home to eat, and then go back to the playground. I'd go home to sleep until 1:00 or 2:00 in the morning. Then I'd go back to play under the lights. That was the only way I could get a court to myself."

He couldn't dance, and the guys in school put him down for not hanging out with them. That hurt. "Some fellows hated me because I seemed to lead such a clean life. That was the hardest thing to accept, the *alienation* from the others. And when they'd smoke and drink and play better than I could, it upset me."

But Jimmy's mother was working on him, in addition to working overtime and Saturdays as a *seamstress*. "She would always say, 'I've been through this. I know what can happen,' " McMillan said. "She had a very rough time. She was trying to see that her children were successful in life."

There was a wealth of good advice at Thomas Jefferson High School, too, where his basketball talent was *obvious* and his 88 average shining for anyone who looked. He had scholarship offers from 150 colleges. People like Coach Sam Beckman encouraged him to think about the educational opportunities in the Ivy League offers, from schools such as Cornell and Columbia, where he could also make a name for himself in basketball. Jim's mother wanted him to go to Columbia, so that was the school he finally chose.

"I felt an *obligation,*" he said. "I'm not that *independent* of my family."

Among the people offering advice there was the voice that told him how much value a Negro could find in an Ivy League *degree,* that there were opportunities opening up if he were *qualified.* "Other people said I couldn't do it," McMillan said. "When *acceptance* came from Columbia, I couldn't believe it. It was better than winning the Most Valuable Player Award."

Columbia was lucky to get Jim McMillan. In his very first year on the team, he led Columbia to the Ivy League championship. He was the leading scorer and the Most Valuable Player in the Madison Square Garden Holiday Festival. But Jim McMillan is not only an outstanding basketball player. He is also an outstanding person, a credit to his family and his school.

—NEWSDAY (Long Island, N.Y.)

CHECK YOUR UNDERSTANDING

1. Another title that would best explain the main idea of this story is:
   (a) The Story of a Basketball Star
   (b) Getting into College
   (c) From South to North
   (d) The Ivy League
2. When Jim McMillan was in the eighth grade
   (a) he was already an outstanding basketball player.

(b) he moved from North Carolina to Brooklyn.

(c) he was unusually small for his age.

(d) he was an excellent dancer.

3. According to Jim McMillan, basketball
   (a) is a game that needs very little practice.
   (b) kept him out of trouble.
   (c) is more important than a good education.
   (d) is a game of luck.

4. In junior high school, Jim McMillan
   (a) was very well-liked.
   (b) smoked and drank.
   (c) did not play basketball.
   (d) was not very popular with the other fellows in school.

5. Jim McMillan chose Columbia University because
   (a) of its educational opportunity.
   (b) of its outstanding basketball team.
   (c) it was the only school to offer him a scholarship.
   (d) he wanted to be independent of his family.

REACHING OUT

1. The fact that one summer Jim McMillan played basketball at one or two o'clock in the morning shows
   (a) he did not study while he went to school.
   (b) he loved the game of basketball.
   (c) he had a job during the day and that was the only time he could play.
   (d) he plays basketball best at night.

2. In his first year on the Columbia team, Jim did *not*
   (a) lead his team to an Ivy League championship.
   (b) become its leading scorer.
   (c) become captain of the team.
   (d) win the Most Valuable Player Award in the Madison Square Garden Holiday Festival.

FIRST THINGS FIRST

Arrange these events in the same order in which they happened to Jim McMillan:
1. The coach at Junior High 64 showed him what a layup was.
2. He won the Most Valuable Player Award at the Madison Square Garden Holiday Festival.
3. He went to school in North Carolina.
4. He won a scholarship to Columbia University.
5. He was a basketball star at Thomas Jefferson High School.
6. He moved to Brooklyn.

IMPROVING YOUR VOCABULARY

In the first column below are the ten words in italics from the story. Pick out the best "story" meaning for each of these words.

1. *obsession* for sweets
(a) weak feeling; (b) strong desire; (c) meeting

2. a *segregated* school — (a) separated by race, religion or other ways; (b) secretly meeting; (c) open for all

3. *alienation* from others — (a) being very friendly; (b) not being very friendly; (c) becoming a citizen

4. work as a *seamstress* — (a) woman who sews for a living; (b) woman who works as a plumber; (c) woman who works on hats

5. an *obvious* truth — (a) difficult to understand; (b) easily understood; (c) going in two directions at once

6. felt an *obligation* — (a) something due to another; (b) something paid for; (c) an insurance policy

7. *independent* of my family — (a) needing help from others; (b) not needing help from others; (c) powerful

8. a college *degree* — (a) diploma for completing difficult levels of education; (b) satisfactory mark; (c) type of learning

9. *qualified* to attend college — (a) wanted; (b) fit and able; (c) unfit for and unable

10. *acceptance* came from Columbia — (a) agreeing to receive; (b) list of new subjects; (c) not agreeing to receive

WORD BUILDING

The word *independent* is used in the story above. It means *not connected with, or controlled by, others.*

Independent is built up from three important word parts: the prefix *in* meaning *not,* the prefix *de* meaning *from,* and the stem *pend* meaning *hang.* If you are independent, then, you don't hang from anyone or anything else: you "swing" alone.

Often, when you see *pend* (or *pens*) in a word, it has the meaning of *hang.*

Example: A *pendant* is a *hanging* object, such as an earring, used as an ornament.

To Do: Match the word in column B to the proper *pend* or *pens* word in column A.

A	**B**
1. a *dependable* friend	(a) added material at end of book
2. *pendulum* on the clock	(b) trustworthy; reliable
3. story full of *suspense*	(c) uncertainty
4. *depend* on me	(d) something hung to swing freely
5. look in the *appendix*	(e) rely for support or aid

A Little Harder: Match, as above.

A	**B**
1. *pending* verdict of the jury	(a) about to happen
2. *suspend* judgment	(b) exclusion from office for a time

200

3. *impending* storm   (c) not decided

4. *interdependent*   (d) hold back
nations of the   (e) needing one another
world

5. *suspension* of the
judge

EXPRESSING YOURSELF

1. The Ivy League has a long tradition of high scholarship, but they have not always attracted the best athletes. If Jim McMillan had asked your advice, why might you have told him to go to Columbia?

2. Interview the basketball coach at your school. Ask him: "What do you look for in an outstanding basketball player?" Draw up at least five more questions to ask him.

3. A parent said, "I don't think it is right for a college to give a boy a scholarship because he is an athlete. Colleges weren't set up for basketball players." Tell why you agree or disagree with that parent.

4. Sam Beckman, Jim's basketball coach at Thomas Jefferson High School, had a great influence on him. Write a paragraph, telling what a good coach should do.

22. HUNTING RATTLESNAKES

THERE ARE MANY UNUSUAL HOBBIES. DO YOU THINK ANY OF YOUR HOBBIES ARE UNUSUAL?

DOES HUNTING RATTLESNAKES SOUND LIKE A PLEASANT WAY TO SPEND YOUR SPARE TIME?

Most women put snakes a little ahead of mice on the fright scale. But Mrs. Carolyn Stevens says,

"A caterpillar gives me more creeps than a snake."

"Snakes make the best pets in the world," said her friend, Mrs. James McGuire. These young housewives and mothers recently returned from the twenty-first *annual* Waynoka Rattlesnake Hunt in Waynoka, Oklahoma.

"It was scary," said the two women, almost in one voice. "But exciting and fun, too," added Mrs. Stevens.

"We had never hunted poisonous snakes before and we wouldn't have *attempted* it alone, but we had three *experienced* herpetologists (snake experts) with us," Mrs. McGuire said.

The three herpetologists included the husbands of the two women and a friend. All three of the men were working or had worked as reptile keepers in zoos.

Telling about the trip, Mrs. Stevens said, "We camped in the Little Sahara State Park in the sand dunes * south of Waynoka. We really didn't see any snakes until the next morning when we crossed the Cimarron River and got to the rocks on top of the cliff. The wind was blowing between 70 and 75 miles an hour, and it was hot, hot, hot! I wrapped one of the snake sacks around my head to keep my hair from blowing in my eyes."

Mrs. McGuire said, "We wore heavy boots and carried snake-bite kits, but our arms were bare because of the heat. A snake can strike only about half the length of its body, but it is a little hard to tell just how long one is when he's all *coiled* up.

"We were by ourselves when we saw the first snake and I didn't have a snake sack. We forgot

* *dunes*—mounds of loose sand.

about the one Carolyn was wearing on her head. We yelled and hollered and screamed and the boys came running," she continued.

"To catch the snakes we use old golf clubs with a hook like a question mark on the end. You always try to stay behind a poisonous snake. If the snake is in the *brush,* it is best to hook it and get it out into the open before trying to bag it.

"Once a snake is in the bag," she went on, "you twist the bag's neck like a rope and then tie a knot above the twist. You carry the sacks at arm's length. And they are plenty heavy! You don't dare let a sack brush against your side; the rattlesnakes can bite right through.

"We hunted all day long and every snake we bagged was bigger than the one before. Every snake we found we brought back and none was injured. You should have heard all twenty of them rattling in the back of the car!" said Mrs. Stevens.

Mr. Stevens pointed out that reptiles don't *adapt* well to *captivity.* "But all our snakes did because of our gentle handling. As soon as they reached the zoo they began eating, which is always a good sign."

The Waynoka Rattlesnake Hunt was *organized* 21 years ago because the snakes were killing cattle. Prizes are offered for such things as the longest and smallest rattlesnakes caught and the greatest number of pounds of rattlesnakes. There is a snake sale and, in the evening, a snake dance.

Stevens and McGuire are childhood friends and began their snake hunting at an early age. Stevens said that as children they could think of no better job than being reptile keepers at the St.

Louis Zoo. "We enjoy studying snakes and *collecting* them, so *naturally* some of this has rubbed off on our wives," he said.

Mrs. McGuire said, "We had a boa constrictor for a pet once. They make such nice pets because they are very quiet. We kept him in my bedroom closet and the kids loved to play with him.

"The boa was really great at parties . . . a real ice-breaker," she added, laughing.

—ST. LOUIS POST-DISPATCH

CHECK YOUR UNDERSTANDING

1. Another title that would best explain the main idea of this story is:
   (a) An Oklahoma Afternoon
   (b) Boa Constrictors
   (c) Hunting
   (d) Snake Story

2. Mrs. Stevens is most afraid of
   (a) snakes.
   (b) mice.
   (c) caterpillars.
   (d) herpetologists.

3. A herpetologist is a
   (a) zoo worker.
   (b) snake expert.
   (c) poisonous snake.
   (d) person with experience.

4. When the women saw the first snake
   (a) they were by themselves.
   (b) they were calm.
   (c) they quickly got it into a bag.
   (d) they ran.

5. The snakes the group caught
   (a) numbered between 70 and 75.
   (b) all died.
   (c) did well because of gentle handling.
   (d) had all killed cattle.

REACHING OUT

1. Mrs. McGuire and Mrs. Stevens did *not* think the Rattlesnake Hunt was
   (a) exciting.
   (b) easy.
   (c) scary.
   (d) fun.

2. The boa constrictor was "great" at Mrs. McGuire's parties because
   (a) the children loved to play with him.
   (b) it gave the guests something to talk about.
   (c) it was in the bedroom closet.
   (d) it was very quiet.

USING WHAT YOU READ

This story tells about steps you should and should not take in capturing poisonous snakes.

206

See how well you have learned what you have just read. For each question below, select the answer THAT IS A MISTAKE made by Herby Tologist when he went out to bag rattlesnakes.

1. When Herby saw the rattlesnake, he
   (a) ran in front of it.
   (b) stayed behind it.
   (c) used an old golf club with a hook to get at the snake.
   (d) tried to get it into a bag.
   What mistake did Herby make?

2. The snake was in the brush so Herby
   (a) tried to hook it and get it into the open.
   (b) tried to bag it right in the brush.
   (c) was very careful.
   (d) stayed behind it.
   What mistake did Herby make?

3. When Herby got the snake in the bag, he
   (a) twisted the neck of the bag like a rope.
   (b) tied a knot above the twist.
   (c) carried the sack at arm's length.
   (d) left the bag open so the snake could breathe.
   What mistake did Herby make?

4. Herby wanted to keep his snakes alive, so he
   (a) fed them.
   (b) brought them to the zoo.
   (c) treated them gently.
   (d) beat them with a stick to make them obedient.
   What mistake did Herby make?

IMPROVING YOUR VOCABULARY

In the first column below are the ten words in italics from the story. Pick out the best ":story" meaning for each of these words.

1. an *annual* event
   (a) every year; (b) every two years; (c) twice a year

2. have *attempted* alone
   (a) teased; (b) tried; (c) spoiled

3. *experienced* workers
   (a) learned by reading; (b) calm; (c) learned by doing

4. a *coiled* snake
   (a) angered; (b) cooked well; (c) wound around in a pile

5. hiding in the *brush*
   (a) woods; (b) field; (c) closet

6. *adapt* to your surroundings
   (a) to be clever about; (b) to move away; (c) to fit or adjust

7. animals in *captivity* in the zoo
   (a) being free; (b) being in prison; (c) being comfortable

8. *organized* 21 years ago
   (a) gotten together; (b) separated; (c) celebrated

9. *collecting* snakes to study them
   (a) bringing together; (b) pulling apart; (c) taking care of

10. *naturally,* it's interesting
    (a) in addition; (b) of course; (c) for example

WORD BUILDING

The word *captivity* is used in the story above. It means *a state of being prisoner.*

Captivity comes from the stem *cap* meaning *to take, seize,* or *hold.* In captivity, a person is taken and held by others.

Usually, when you see *cap* in a word, it has the meaning of *take, hold,* or *seize. Cap* may appear as *cep* or *cip.*

Examples: To *captivate* means to *take* or get the attention or affection of.

To *except* means to *take* out or exclude.

To *participate* means to *take* part in.

To Do: Match the word in column B to the proper *cap* word in column A.

A	B
1. *capacity* of the room	(a) taking by force
2. *captor* of the soldier	(b) skilled; able to do well
3. a *capable* secretary	(c) roomy; spacious
4. *capture* the city	(d) a person who takes another as a prisoner
5. *capacious* house	(e) ability to hold or receive

A Little Harder: Match the word in column B to the proper *cep* word in column A.

A	**B**
1. *accept* the award	(a) misleading act or statement making a person believe what is not true
2. *deception* of her parent	
3. *reception* of a letter	(b) easily influenced or affected by
4. *susceptible* to colds	(c) agree to take
5. *exceptional* ability	(d) taking or getting
	(e) unusual; outstanding

EXPRESSING YOURSELF

1. "Snakes make the best pets in the world," said Mrs. James McGuire. What is your favorite pet and why?

2. Hunting rattlesnakes is a dangerous hobby unless you know what you are doing. Here are other dangerous hobbies or sports. Choose one you might like to try and tell why.
   (a) scuba diving
   (b) mountain climbing
   (c) racing automobiles
   (d) raising a pet ocelot
   (e) big-game hunting

3. Imagine that you received a special-delivery package containing a live snake. Tell of the

thoughts which might go through your mind and describe the action you would take.

4. Waynoka, Oklahoma, sponsors a contest with a prize for the person who captures the most rattlesnakes. Tell about a contest you would like to sponsor.

23. SHOOTING WILD ANIMALS WITH A MOVIE CAMERA

WANTED: YOUNG MAN WITH CAMERA TO SHOOT WILD ANIMALS IN THE JUNGLE.

WOULD YOU ANSWER THIS AD?

"The best way to look at a lion is from a distance," says Murl Deusing. He speaks not from *cowardice* but from long experience photographing

wildlife in its natural state. "And the only way to photograph wildlife in its natural state is not to let it know you are there," he says.

"We use a telephoto lens, but even so, things can get a little rough at times," Deusing said when he was in town to talk about his new television series.

"You have to be able to sniff out the way a lion feels, at 300 feet," he said. "You shoot (I mean film) from an open jeep with the motor turned off. This leaves you wide open. Lions are slow to anger, but when you see one's ears flatten back, his tail straighten and begin to twitch, you'd better get out.

"I knew a hunter," Deusing continued, "who could look at a lion and tell whether it was dangerous. Not all of them are. We've had lions moving along next to our open jeep quite *harmlessly*. But you mustn't wave at them or talk too much. Getting close is just a matter of *judgment,* and sometimes you judge wrong.

"One morning we *located* a big old male lion on the kill. We were doing some good shooting until one of the trackers started coughing. The coughing *disturbed* the lion who was 500 or 600 feet away from our parked jeep. That isn't much space between you and an angry lion. He turned and began to come at us. We started the jeep and took off. When we got to a speed of about 35 miles an hour he began to lose ground and quit the chase."

Deusing has been charged by water buffalo and chased up trees by rhinos. If he had to choose, he would prefer to be *pursued* by a water buffalo. Rhinos, it seems, are unpredictable as well as *ferocious*.

"A rhino will explode, with no warning. It charges fast and turns like a polo pony," he said. "Rhinos are trouble. They make you wonder why you got into this business."

If a rhino—sharpening his tusk on the tree trunk a few feet away from the seat of Deusing's pants—made him wonder how he got into this business, he could have blamed it on his father.

As the son of a Milwaukee photographer, Murl Deusing learned as a boy the art of shooting a sharp, clear picture. Photography became more than just a hobby for Deusing; it became an obsession.

Since his graduation from college, Deusing has been a traveler, speaker, wildlife photographer and director of a scientific society. His television *career* began in St. Louis when he was asked to make the "What's New" series for National Education Television. It was well received by children and parents alike.

Next, he filmed a travel series in which he asked guest explorers the same kinds of questions an *audience* would ask. Just as he has learned to tell the way a lion feels from the *behavior* of its tail, he has learned to spot the tall tales * from the behavior of the explorers he talks with.

"I have to admit that explorers as a group have been known to stretch the truth a bit here and there," he said with a grin. "As one of my favorites, a former lumberjack turned explorer, says when you ask him if a story is really true, 'Well, Murl, let's just say it's truer than most of my stories.'"

—ST. LOUIS POST-DISPATCH

CHECK YOUR UNDERSTANDING

1. Another title that would best explain the main idea of this story is:
   (a) The Lion and the Rhinoceros
   (b) Photography
   (c) Photographing Wildlife
   (d) Television Explorers
2. According to Deusing, lions
   (a) all act alike.
   (b) are not dangerous.
   (c) like to be photographed.
   (d) don't get angry easily.
3. According to Deusing, rhinos
   (a) are less dangerous than water buffalo.
   (b) are gentle.
   (c) are ferocious and unpredictable.
   (d) are more dangerous than lions.

* *tall tales*—exaggerated stories.

215

4. According to the story, the television program "What's New" was
  - (a) disliked by children.
  - (b) disliked by children and parents.
  - (c) liked by both children and parents.
  - (d) liked by children, but not by parents.

5. Deusing thinks that explorers on television
  - (a) sometimes stretch the truth a bit.
  - (b) always tell the truth.
  - (c) never tell the truth.
  - (d) are all former lumberjacks.

REACHING OUT

1. Deusing has *not* been
  - (a) a photographer.
  - (b) a president of a university.
  - (c) a traveler.
  - (d) a performer on a television series.

2. The statement in paragraph 7 that rhinos turn like polo ponies means that rhinos
  - (a) are clumsy.
  - (b) move fast.
  - (c) are easily fooled.
  - (d) are horses.

WHAT'S THE REASON?

Good readers are good detectives. They see *why* things happen. See if you can find the right *why* to complete each of these statements.

1. Murl Deusing thinks you should stay far away from a lion because
   (a) he knows from his experience that lions are dangerous.
   (b) he is a coward.
   (c) lions look better from a distance.
   (d) lions are cowards.

2. Deusing says that when you see a lion's tail straighten and begin to twitch, you'd better get out because
   (a) his ears will flatten back.
   (b) that is a sign that the lion is angry.
   (c) the lion's tail is dangerous.
   (d) Deusing wants to take the lion's picture.

3. The big, old lion in paragraph 5 attacked Deusing because
   (a) a tracker's coughing disturbed the lion.
   (b) all lions will attack photographers.
   (c) the lion noticed Deusing's camera.
   (d) the lion was frightened by the jeep.

4. The lion stopped chasing the jeep because
   (a) Deusing was taking his picture.
   (b) the jeep was about to run the lion over.
   (c) he was too old, and got tired.
   (d) he saw he couldn't catch the jeep.

IMPROVING YOUR VOCABULARY

In the first column below are the ten words in italics from the story. Pick out the best "story" meaning for each of these words.

1. frozen by his *cowardice*   (a) full of courage; (b) lack of courage; (c) over-weight
2. moving near us *harmlessly*   (a) dangerously; (b) funny; (c) safely
3. a matter of *judgment*   (a) wishing; (b) opinion; (c) fact
4. *located* a big lion   (a) found the exact place; (b) lost; (c) captured
5. *disturbed* by a cough   (a) bothered; (b) toppled; (c) disgusted
6. *pursued* by a water buffalo   (a) split; (b) chased; (c) eaten
7. *ferocious* rhinos   (a) adult; (b) frightened; (c) fierce
8. successful television *career*   (a) life's work; (b) repair man; (c) family show
9. a large *audience*   (a) a place where people meet; (b) people gathered to hear and see; (c) a special program
10. the *behavior* of a lion   (a) conduct; (b) size; (c) feelings

---

WORD BUILDING

The word *located* is used in the story above. It means *found the exact position, or place, of.*

Located is built up from the stem *loc* meaning *place.* Usually, when you see *loc* in a word, it has the meaning of *place.*

Example: A *locality* is a *place.*

To Do: Match the word in column B to the proper *loc* word in column A.

A	B
1. *local* election	(a) railroad engine
2. *location* on a hill	(b) having to do with a particular place
3. *relocate* in a new area	(c) put out of joint
4. *locomotive* coming into view	(d) position
5. *dislocate* a shoulder	(e) change one's position or place

A Little Harder: Match, as above.

A	B
1. *locale* of the movie	(a) moving from place to place
2. *allocate* money	(b) place; setting
3. means of *locomotion*	(c) in a particular area
4. *localize* the battle	(d) give out; distribute
5. newspaper distributed *locally*	(e) limit to a particular place

---

EXPRESSING YOURSELF

1. It sounds exciting and glamorous to photograph wild jungle animals. Why, however, aside from the danger, would most people refuse to take such a job? Tell why you would, or would not, like to join Murl Deusing.

2. People are fascinated by a camera from the moment they discover that they can record life without words. Tell about three scenes that you would like to photograph.

3. "A picture is worth a thousand words." Tell why you agree or disagree.

4. Bring your camera to school. Take pictures of your classmates in their favorite poses. Then after you have the film developed, have each classmate write a brief biography of himself to accompany his picture.

5. Deusing describes the signs that tell us when a lion is angry. (For example, his ears flatten back, and his tail straightens and begins to twitch.) Write a paragraph about a relative or a friend and tell about the signs that tell you when he is beginning to get angry.

6. Deusing says that explorers like to stretch the truth. Why would they do that? Tell about a recent story you have told where you exaggerated a little.

24. DANNY FERNANDEZ

A BABY CARRIAGE ROLLS INTO THE STREET AS A TRUCK RUMBLES DOWN ON IT. SUDDENLY A YOUNG MAN DARTS OUT OF NOWHERE, PUSHES THE CARRIAGE OUT OF THE WAY, BUT GETS HIT BY THE TRUCK. WHAT MADE HIM RISK HIS LIFE?

IN OUR STORY, DANNY FERNANDEZ RISKED HIS LIFE TO SAVE HIS ARMY BUDDIES? WOULD YOU HAVE ACTED AS DANNY DID?

CUCHI, South Vietnam, Feb. 19—Danny Fernandez was one of those *rare* young men who are looked up to by their *comrades*—quiet, *competent,* unselfish, cheerful, the type chosen as president of the senior class.

When he died yesterday, a few months short of his twenty-second birthday, he was a rifleman in the United States 25th Infantry Division, and everyone who had known him *mourned.*

They would have felt the loss in any case, but there was a deeper *grief* because Danny Fernandez chose death by throwing his body across a live Vietcong grenade to save four of his comrades.

The report at headquarters might have added one fact—that Danny Fernandez has been *recommended* by his division for the Medal of Honor.

He was not a career soldier. He used to joke with his friends that he was in the Army for 3 years because he had flipped a coin with his draft board and lost. Actually, he had joined the Army for 3 years.

His father is a rancher, and Danny had hoped to settle in Texas to do the same thing. He had hoped to marry a girl named Becky some day. He had hoped to have a string of horses because he liked riding more than anything else.

While he was in the Army, he wanted to be a good soldier. In Hawaii, where the 25th was *stationed* before coming to Cuchi, he spent hours reading over Army training books.

His platoon leader, Second Lieutenant Joseph V. Dorso of Norwalk, Conn., called him "the type of guy I could always count on, no matter what the situation." Sergeant David M. Thompson of Bellmawr, N.J., who used to go sky-diving with him in Hawaii, said simply, "Danny was my best friend."

The members of his squad looked upon Danny as a father confessor. Even those who were older than he called him "Uncle Dan" and went to him with their troubles and *complaints*.

Danny Fernandez had been to Vietnam once before, as a volunteer machine gunner on an Army helicopter. So it was not surprising that he was one of 16 men who volunteered for a patrol sent out from Cuchi just after midnight yesterday.

At about 7 A.M., as the patrol lay in wait in a jungle clearing, the Vietcong opened up with machine-gun fire. Five men, including Specialist Fernandez, were pinned down in an area no bigger than a living room. Then a grenade fired from a rifle by one of the Vietcong landed beside Danny's leg. He got up on all fours, trying to escape, but he hit the grenade with his ankle, knocking it to within a few feet of two men who had been wounded.

Without waiting a second, Specialist Fernandez shouted, "Move out!" and threw himself onto the grenade. It blew up under him, and a machine-gun bullet hit him seconds later. When the others reached him, he was still *conscious.* The men made a litter from their shirts and bamboo poles and dragged Danny to an open area where a helicopter could land.

The last man he talked with was Sgt. Ruben Perkins of Nashville, Tenn., with whom he had shared a foxhole * on the *dreary* plain of Cuchi.

"I'm sorry," he said to Sergeant Perkins. "Someone else is going to have to take care of you because old Dan has got to go now."

He died on the helicopter.

"He was the kind of person you want yourself to be," Dave Masingale, the platoon's medic, said. "You know, we'd all like to say to ourselves that we would do the same thing in the same situation. I wonder . . ."

—NEW YORK TIMES

CHECK YOUR UNDERSTANDING

1. Another title which best expresses the main idea of this story is:

* A *foxhole* is a hole dug in the ground by a soldier and used by him for cover when the fighting starts.

(a) Beyond the Call of Duty
(b) The Grenade
(c) A President of the Senior Class
(d) The Helicopter
2. The patrol with Specialist Fernandez
   (a) was attacked by five men.
   (b) had seven members.
   (c) couldn't move because of enemy fire.
   (d) escaped safely.
3. Danny Fernandez was called "Uncle Dan" by
   (a) all the men.
   (b) his platoon leader.
   (c) the children.
   (d) the older men.
4. Dave Masingale, the platoon medic, wondered if
   (a) he would be safe.
   (b) Danny would live.
   (c) he would have the courage to give up his life.
   (d) Danny would do it again.
5. The last person who spoke to Danny Fernandez was
   (a) Sergeant Perkins.
   (b) the medic.
   (c) Lieutenant Dorso.
   (d) Sergeant Thompson.

REACHING OUT

1. A word that would best describe Specialist Fernandez is:
   (a) proud.
   (b) brave.

(c) foolish.

(d) weak.

2. When Danny Fernandez said that he flipped a coin with his draft board and lost, his mood was

(a) serious.

(b) angry.

(c) nasty.

(d) humorous.

FIRST THINGS FIRST

Arrange these events in the order in which they happened to Danny Fernandez.

1. He served as a machine gunner in an Army helicopter.
2. He enjoyed riding horses in Texas.
3. He was carried to a helicopter.
4. He was shipped to Cuchi.
5. He was awarded the Medal of Honor.
6. He was blown up by a grenade.
7. He wanted to go on a special patrol outside of Cuchi.

WHAT'S THE REASON?

Good readers are good detectives. They see *why* things happen. See if you can find the correct *why* to complete each of these statements.

1. Danny Fernandez dived on top of the grenade because

(a) he didn't see it.

(b) he was trying to escape.

(c) he wanted to save the lives of two men he had accidentally put in danger.

(d) he had special clothing to protect him.

2. Danny Fernandez could be counted on because
   (a) his platoon leader said so.
   (b) he performed his duties with responsibility.
   (c) he loved horses.
   (d) his men called him Uncle Dan.

3. Specialist Danny Fernandez was awarded the Medal of Honor because
   (a) he was Sgt. Thompson's best man.
   (b) he gave his life to save the lives of other men.
   (c) he was in the Army.
   (d) his comrades liked him.

4. Danny Fernandez hoped to work on a ranch because
   (a) he had promised to help his father.
   (b) his girl lived there.
   (c) it was outdoor work.
   (d) he loved horses.

IMPROVING YOUR VOCABULARY

In the first column below are the ten words in italics from the story. Pick out the best "story" meaning for each of these words.

1. *rare* young men (a) unusual; (b) uncooked; (c) rude

2. to save two *comrades* (a) friends; (b) enemies; (c) cousins

3. a *competent* person (a) opposing; (b) capable; (c) confused

4. *mourned* for Danny	(a) was sad for; (b) searched for; (c) spoke for
5. felt a deeper *grief*	(a) strong belief; (b) great sadness; (c) hate
6. *recommended* for a medal	(a) spoke against; (b) performed; (c) spoke in favor of
7. *stationed* in Hawaii	(a) landed at; (b) placed for duty; (c) flew away
8. their troubles and *complaints*	(a) statements of blame; (b) crying in pain; (c) bad language
9. still *conscious* after the grenade exploded	(a) very hard; (b) unhurt; (c) awake
10. the *dreary* plain of Cuchi	(a) wet; (b) without cheer; (c) dry

---

WORD BUILDING

The word *stationed* is used in the story above. It means *placed*.

Stationed comes from the stem *sta,* which means *stand*. If you are stationed at a particular place, you stand, or stay, there.

Usually, when you see *sta* in a word, it has the meaning of *stand*.

Example: *Static* means *standing* still, not moving.

To Do: Match the word in column B to the proper *sta* word in column A.

A	**B**
1. *stabilize* the situation	(a) far-off (b) standing still

228

2. *distant* place   (c) steady; make firm
3. *instant* action   (d) immediate
4. *obstacle* to success   (e) something in the way
5. *stationary* position

A Little Harder: Match, as above.

A	**B**
1. *constant* friendship	(a) height
2. sticky *substance*	(b) unchanging; faithful
3. *substantial* salary increase	(c) fact; event
	(d) material; what a thing is made of
4. great in *stature*	
5. a strange *circumstance*	(e) large; important

EXPRESSING YOURSELF

1. Dave Masingale, the platoon's medic, wondered whether he could have done what Danny did. Could you have done it?

2. Some men might do as Danny Fernandez did. Most men would not. How can you tell whether one of your friends is the type who would give up his life to save others?

3. When a Medal of Honor is presented, the general always reads a statement telling what the soldier had done to earn that great award. Write such a paragraph describing Danny Fernandez's bravery.

4. Danny was the type of person that people went to with their troubles. Tell about a person you know who is sympathetic the way Danny was.

229

25. CHILDREN'S STREET PLAY CHANGES

CITY CHILDREN OFTEN MUST MAKE THE STREET THEIR PLAYGROUND.

WHICH OF THE STREET GAMES DESCRIBED HERE COULD BE YOUR FAVORITE?

The stickball player hit the ball onto a roof on East Ninth Street, near Avenue A. None of the players bothered to get it. Instead, the boys chipped in 25 cents and bought another ball. The day before, five balls had been hit onto roofs. They had all been left there.

"We don't usually chase a ball on the roof," Michael Pinto said, "unless we don't have any money. Then we go up on the roofs and look around for balls."

Less than two *decades* ago, a boy in a poor, or lower-middle-class, neighborhood of the city would have climbed a fire escape or *descended* into a sewer to get a 10-cent ball.

This is one of the number of changes in the city's street games. One major change seems to be the disappearance of punchball. In a trip through Manhattan the other day, an observer could not find one punchball game. Any boys who were questioned knew nothing about the game, one of the city's favorite street sports a *generation* ago.

Punchball, generally played with the same pink ball so common today, had rules very *similar* to baseball. Sometimes the ball was pitched to the player "at bat" on one bounce. Sometimes he hit it himself after bouncing it or throwing it into the air.

Punchball has been made more *familiar* lately by Bill Cosby, the entertainer. He has used the game as a subject for one of his records. Mr. Cosby is a former star athlete at Temple University. He tells of the two-sewer hitter, meaning a player who could drive the ball far into the outfield, since the manhole covers were usually used for home plate and for second base.

Stoopball, however, has survived with the rules of the game changing according to the layout of the block and the space available.

On East 118th Street, near Lexington Avenue, for instance, the number of bases *varies* with the number of players. The ball is bounced off a stoop and then fielded as the thrower runs to a base. One type of stoopball does not involve any base running. The ball is merely bounced off the stoop. The aim is to get it past one, two or three fielders in the street. If the ball is caught on the fly, it is an out, but if it gets by one fielder it is a single, two fielders, a double and so on.

Basketballs are in use in streets, mainly to practice dribbling. The games are for the playgrounds. Tops show no sign of disappearing, and youngsters still try to *scoop* up a spinning top on the palm of the hand and keep it turning. For girls, hopscotch is still a *popular* game.

Handball hangs on as a street game. But mostly it is played on playground courts instead of against apartment house, factory or garage walls. And even the handball played in the street is now the milder form, known as "Chinese" handball, in which the player has to hit the ball so that it bounces once before it reaches the wall.

Some of the fun has gone out of street sports since the disappearance of stickball games between different blocks. One *adolescent* in East Harlem, when asked if he had played against teams from nearby blocks, looked *astonished*.

"Why should we play another block?" he asked.

Perhaps one of the most famous and most successful stickball players was Willie Mays, the center-fielder for the San Francisco Giants. After starting his professional baseball career with the Giants in New York, Willie would frequently break into a stickball lineup on the streets of Harlem.

—NEW YORK TIMES

CHECK YOUR UNDERSTANDING

1. Another title that would best explain the main idea of this story is:
   (a) Big-City Street Games
   (b) Stickball Games
   (c) Willie Mays
   (d) Famous Games

2. A contest that once was popular but is no longer is
   (a) handball.
   (b) basketball.
   (c) stickball between blocks.
   (d) Chinese handball.

3. A famous person who enjoyed playing stickball after he became a professional is
   (a) the writer of the story.
   (b) Michael Pinto.
   (c) Willie Mays.
   (d) Bill Cosby.

4. A two-sewer hitter is
   (a) Bill Cosby.
   (b) Willie Mays.
   (c) a person who could hit a ball a distance of two manhole covers.
   (d) a person who could quickly run the distance between two manhole covers.

5. In stoopball, if the ball gets by three fielders it is
   (a) a double.
   (b) an out.
   (c) a triple.
   (d) a single.

REACHING OUT

1. Teams from different city blocks no longer play against each other because
   (a) there are no youngsters around.
   (b) there is no interest anymore.
   (c) parents forbid them.
   (d) there are too many cars in the streets.
2. Youngsters in Harlem don't chase balls on roofs because
   (a) they have money to buy new ones.
   (b) they have an unlimited supply.
   (c) there are none there.
   (d) they don't play in the streets.

NAME THAT GAME

stoopball
Chinese handball
handball
punchball
basketball
hopscotch
tops

Which of these games do each of the following statements describe?

1. If the ball gets past one fielder, it is a single.
2. The players can move with the ball only by dribbling it.
3. The ball must bounce before reaching the wall.
4. One of the tricks is to scoop up the toy while it's spinning.

5. The ball must hit the wall on the fly.
6. The special court for this game is six or eight numbered boxes.
7. The player must use his hand in place of a bat.

WHAT DID YOU SAY?

Match the meaning in column B to the expression in column A.

A	**B**
1. on the fly	(a) shared
2. off a stoop	(b) without a bounce
3. chipped in	(c) bounce the ball
4. dribble	(d) from the steps in front of a house

IMPROVING YOUR VOCABULARY

In the first column below are the ten words in italics from the story. Pick out the best "story" meaning for each of these words.

1. two *decades* ago (a) periods of 10 years; (b) periods of 50 years; (c) periods of 100 years

2. *descended* into sewers (a) walked by; (b) went up; (c) went down

3. a *generation* ago (a) about 30 years, or all the people born during that period; (b) power plants; (c) generals of the army

4. rules *similar* to baseball   (a) changing; (b) different; (c) alike

5. a *familiar* face   (a) special; (b) known to all; (c) missing

6. *varies* with the number of players   (a) adds on; (b) changes; (c) loses

7. to *scoop* up a spinning top   (a) to take up; (b) to bend down; (c) to pull away

8. a *popular* game   (a) liked by students; (b) about a tree; (c) liked by most people

9. *adolescent* years   (a) teen-age; (b) elderly; (c) infant

10. *astonished* by the question   (a) very surprised; (b) excited; (c) frightened

---

WORD BUILDING

The word *generation* is used in the story above. It means *all the people born at about the same time.*

Generation comes from the stem *gen* which means *a kind* or *a race.* A *generation* consists of people of the *same kind of age.*

When you see *gen* in a word, it usually means *kind, race, nation, produce,* or *give birth to.*

Example: A *generator* is a machine that *produces* electricity.

To Do: Match the word in column B to the proper *gen* word in column A.

A	**B**
1. a *generous* act	(a) widespread; common
2. a *genuine* Rembrandt painting	(b) a person with great mental ability

236

3. *gentle* rain from Heaven

4. *general* agreement

5. a scientific *genius*

(c) true; real

(d) mild; moderate

(e) unselfish; willing to give or share

A Little Harder: Match, as above.

A	**B**
1. *generate* energy	(a) kindly
2. *degenerate* into a mob	(b) grow worse; lose good qualities
3. *regenerate* a limb	(c) bring into being again
4. *congenital* disease	(d) produce; bring into being
5. a *genial* person	(e) existing at birth

EXPRESSING YOURSELF

1. Imagine that a large park is to be built in your neighborhood and the city planners have asked teen-agers to tell them how the space in the park should be used. Draw a diagram or describe your ideas in paragraph form.

2. Everyone has a favorite outdoor game that he has played. Tell about your favorite game.

3. In this story there are several expressions that were popular in the street games played by youngsters. For example, "on the fly," and "off a stoop," are two. What other interesting expressions about outdoor games can you list?

4. Write a paragraph about the high point of your athletic career.

REVIEW OF LESSONS 21-25

IMPROVING YOUR VOCABULARY

Choose the correct meaning for each of the words in the first column. (The number in parentheses after each word is the number of the lesson where the word first appeared.)

1. acceptance (21)   (a) receiving what is offered; (b) giving away; (c) taking back

2. adapt (22)   (a) clever; (b) borrow; (c) adjust to

3. adolescent (25)   (a) infant; (b) teen-age; (c) elderly

4. alienation (21)   (a) making friends; (b) loss of friends; (c) respecting parents

238

5. annual (22)   (a) yearly; (b) monthly; (c) daily

6. astonished (25)   (a) very surprised; (b) very happy; (c) very proud

7. attempted (22)   (a) failed; (b) worked; (c) tried

8. audience (23)   (a) special event; (b) place where people meet; (c) people gathered to hear and see

9. behavior (23)   (a) feeling; (b) mood; (c) conduct

10. brush (22)   (a) woods; (b) jungle; (c) desert

11. captivity (22)   (a) being safe; (b) being in prison; (c) being free

12. career (23)   (a) a vacation; (b) a large ship; (c) a profession

13. coiled (22)   (a) wound up; (b) caught; (c) losing

14. collecting (22)   (a) meeting; (b) gathering; (c) losing

15. competent (24)   (a) trying; (b) unfit; (c) able

16. complaints (24)   (a) statements of blame; (b) statements of praise; (c) swearing

17. comrades (24)   (a) friends; (b) raiders; (c) heroes

18. conscious (24)   (a) asleep; (b) dead; (c) awake

19. cowardice (23)   (a) being strong; (b) being afraid; (c) being ill

20. decades (25)	(a) periods of 10 years; (b) periods of 20 years; (c) periods of 50 years
21. degree (21)	(a) map; (b) diploma; (c) vocation
22. descend (25)	(a) go up; (b) go straight; (c) go down
23. disturbed (23)	(a) troubled; (b) separated; (c) given out
24. dreary (24)	(a) dreamy; (b) dull; (c) exciting
25. experienced (22)	(a) trained by doing; (b) graduated; (c) overworked
26. familiar (25)	(a) known to all; (b) related; (c) forgotten
27. ferocious (23)	(a) tame; (b) dumb; (c) savage
28. generation (25)	(a) electric power plant; (b) about 30 years, or all the people born during that period; (c) section
29. grief (24)	(a) great joy; (b) great sorrow; (c) a male giraffe
30. harmlessly (23)	(a) without damaging; (b) hurting; (c) twisting
31. independent (21)	(a) safe; (b) kept out; (c) free
32. judgment (23)	(a) news; (b) jury; (c) opinion
33. located (23)	(a) lost; (b) followed; (c) found
34. mourned (24)	(a) was glad for; (b) was sad for; (c) was sick about

240

35. naturally (22)	(a) of course; (b) maybe; (c) possibly
36. obligation (21)	(a) payment; (b) duty; (c) loan
37. obvious (22)	(a) not to be doubted; (b) to be doubted; (c) foolish
38. organized (22)	(a) carried; (b) put into order; (c) replaced
39. obsession (21)	(a) a strong troubling feeling; (b) a long meeting; (c) a decision
40. popular (25)	(a) a tall tree; (b) liked by most people; (c) crowded
41. pursued (23)	(a) took to court; (b) stole; (c) followed
42. qualified (21)	(a) fit and able; (b) unfit and unable; (c) joined by
43. rare (24)	(a) ordinary; (b) baked; (c) unusual
44. recommended (24)	(a) hired; (b) joined the army; (c) suggested for promotion
45. seamstress (21)	(a) a dress; (b) a woman who sews; (c) a sewing machine
46. segregated (21)	(a) separated; (b) connected; (c) sweetened
47. scoop (25)	(a) brush away; (b) crack; (c) take up
48. similar (25)	(a) different; (b) much the same; (c) shiny
49. stationed (24)	(a) replaced; (b) stopped; (c) placed

50. varies (25)   (a) paints; (b) changes; (c) weighs

WORD-BUILDING PARTS

Match the word in column B to the proper word-building part in column A.

A	B
1. *cap* (22)	(a) hanging
2. *loc* (23)	(b) stand
3. *sta* (24)	(c) take; seize
4. *gen* (25)	(d) a kind
5. *pend, pens* (21)	(e) place

WORD-BUILDING VOCABULARY

Choose the best meaning for each of the words in the first column.

1. appendix (21)   (a) beginning of a book; (b) index; (c) material at the end of a book

2. capable (22)   (a) skilled; (b) unskilled; (c) full

3. capacity (22)   (a) forgetting; (b) capital city; (c) ability to hold or receive

4. capture (22)   (a) seize; (b) release; (c) defend

5. dependable (21)   (a) unable to support; (b) can be relied on for support; (c) workable

6. dislocate (23)   (a) put out of joint; (b) find; (c) disappear

7. distant (24)   (a) sharp; (b) near; (c) far-off

8. general (25)   (a) not common; (b) widespread; (c) ordinary

9. generous (25)   (a) special; (b) selfish; (c) unselfish

10. genuine (25)   (a) real; (b) fake; (c) leather

11. genius (25)   (a) strong person; (b) weak person; (c) very smart person

12. instant (24)   (a) immediate; (b) temporary; (c) last

13. locale (23)   (a) rapid; (b) particular place; (c) slow train

14. location (23)   (a) kindness; (b) position; (c) health rest

15. obstacle (24)   (a) sight; (b) bridge; (c) something in the way

16. pendulum (21)   (a) something taking time; (b) something swinging freely; (c) cereal

17. relocate (23)   (a) move to another place; (b) fill up; (c) advance

18. stabilize (24)   (a) loosen; (b) make firm; (c) weaken

19. stationary (24)   (a) moving; (b) standing still; (c) paper

20. suspense (21)   (a) uncertainty; (b) certainty; (c) thoughtfulness

A Little Harder: Match the meaning in column B to the proper word in column A.

A	B
1. constant (24)	(a) hold back
2. deception (22)	(b) not decided
3. exceptional (22)	(c) needing one another
4. generate (25)	(d) outstanding
5. interdependent (25)	(e) misleading act
	(f) setting
6. locale (23)	(g) moving from place to place
7. locomotion (23)	
8. pending (21)	(h) faithful
9. substance (24)	(i) material
10. suspend (21)	(j) produce